I0428084

Pipeline Accident Report

Storage Tank Explosion and Fire in Glenpool, Oklahoma
April 7, 2003

NTSB/PAR-04/02
PB2004-916502
Notation 7666
Adopted October 13, 2004

National Transportation Safety Board
490 L'Enfant Plaza, S.W.
Washington, D.C. 20594

National Transportation Safety Board. 2004. *Storage Tank Explosion and Fire in Glenpool, Oklahoma, April 7, 2003.* **Pipeline Accident Report NTSB/PAR-04/02. Washington, DC.**

Abstract: About 8:55 p.m., central daylight time, on April 7, 2003, an 80,000-barrel storage tank at ConocoPhillips Company's Glenpool South tank farm in Glenpool, Oklahoma, exploded and burned as it was being filled with diesel. Gasoline had been removed from the tank earlier in the day. The resulting fire burned for about 21 hours and damaged two other storage tanks in the area. The cost of the accident was $2,357,483. There were no injuries or fatalities. Nearby residents were evacuated, and schools were closed for 2 days.

The safety issues identified in this accident are tank operations, including switch loading, at the ConocoPhillips Company tank farm; the adequacy of emergency planning and emergency response by ConocoPhillips and American Electric Power; and the adequacy of Federal regulations and industry standards for emergency planning.

As a result of its investigation of this accident, the Safety Board makes safety recommendations to the Research and Special Programs Administration, ConocoPhillips Company, American Electric Power, the American Society of Mechanical Engineers, and the Institute of Electrical and Electronics Engineers.

Contents

Executive Summary

On April 7, 2003, at about 8:55 p.m., central daylight time, an 80,000-barrel storage tank at ConocoPhillips Company's Glenpool South tank farm in Glenpool, Oklahoma, exploded and burned as it was being filled with diesel. The tank, designated tank 11, had previously contained gasoline, which had been removed from the tank earlier in the day. The tank contained between 7,397 and 7,600 barrels of diesel at the time of the explosion. The resulting fire burned for about 21 hours and damaged two other storage tanks in the area. The cost of the accident, including emergency response, environmental remediation, evacuation, lost product, property damage, and claims, was $2,357,483. There were no injuries or fatalities. Nearby residents were evacuated, and schools were closed for 2 days.

The National Transportation Safety Board determines that the probable cause of the April 7, 2003, storage tank explosion and fire in Glenpool, Oklahoma, was ignition of a flammable fuel-air mixture within the tank by a static electricity discharge due to the improper manner in which ConocoPhillips Company conducted tank operations. Contributing to the extent of the property damage and the magnitude of the impact on the local community was the failure of American Electric Power employees to recognize the risk the tank fire posed to the nearby power lines and take effective emergency action.

The safety issues identified during the investigation of this accident are as follows:

- Tank operations, including switch loading, at the ConocoPhillips tank farm.

- The adequacy of emergency planning and emergency response by ConocoPhillips Company and American Electric Power.

- The adequacy of Federal regulations and industry standards for emergency planning.

As a result of its investigation of this accident, the National Transportation Safety Board makes safety recommendations to the Research and Special Programs Administration, ConocoPhillips Company, American Electric Power, the American Society of Mechanical Engineers, and the Institute of Electrical and Electronics Engineers.

Factual Information

Accident Synopsis

On April 7, 2003, at about 8:55 p.m., central daylight time,[1] an 80,000-barrel storage tank at ConocoPhillips Company's (ConocoPhillips) Glenpool South tank farm in Glenpool, Oklahoma, exploded and burned as it was being filled with diesel. The tank, designated tank 11, had previously contained gasoline, which had been removed from the tank earlier in the day. The tank contained between 7,397 and 7,600 barrels of diesel at the time of the explosion. The resulting fire burned for about 21 hours and damaged two other storage tanks in the area. The cost of the accident, including emergency response, environmental remediation, evacuation, lost product, property damage, and claims, was $2,357,483. There were no injuries or fatalities. Nearby residents were evacuated, and schools were closed for 2 days.

Accident Narrative

Tank 11 contained about 8,710 barrels[2] of gasoline on the afternoon of the accident. The ConocoPhillips operator who was on duty at the time of the accident stated that when she reported for work at Glenpool Terminal at about 3:30 p.m.[3] on April 7, 2003, a transfer of gasoline from tank 11 at Glenpool South tank farm, a nearby ConocoPhillips facility, to tankage at Glenpool Terminal, was in progress. Explorer Pipeline Company (Explorer) was scheduled to deliver a batch of diesel into tank 11 about 8:30 p.m., and before that time, the operator would need to complete the transfer of gasoline to Glenpool Terminal and remove the gasoline that remained in the manifold piping and the piping to tank 11. The gasoline from the piping would be transferred to tank 12 at Glenpool South tank farm.[4]

---

[1]   Unless otherwise specified, the times used in this report are central daylight time.

[2]   A *barrel* is a liquid measure that, for petroleum, is equal to 42 U.S. gallons.

[3]   Times in this section are from interviews with ConocoPhillips, Explorer Pipeline Company, and American Electric Power personnel, ConocoPhillips and Explorer Pipeline computer data, the Glenpool fire captain's summary report, the Glenpool police daily radio log, ConocoPhillips incident tracking notification data, and the Explorer Pipeline Company batch end report.

[4]   The diesel delivery normally would have been to tank 8, but because of scheduling considerations, the naphtha in tank 8 had not been shipped, making it necessary to empty tank 11 in preparation for the scheduled diesel delivery. In 2002 and 2003, tank 11 was used to store naphtha, toluene, gasoline, and diesel. *Naphtha* is a petroleum distillate used as a paint solvent, cleaning fluid, and blendstock in gasoline production. *Toluene* is a petroleum distillate used as an octane booster in fuel and as a solvent in paints and paint thinners, rubber, printing, adhesives, cosmetics, fingernail polish, lacquers, leather tanning, disinfectants, and perfumes.

The piping system at the Glenpool South tank farm allowed products to be delivered to and received from Explorer's facility, which was northwest of and adjacent to the ConocoPhillips tank farm. (See figure 1.) The piping system also allowed products to be delivered to and received from the ConocoPhillips Glenpool Terminal (also identified by ConocoPhillips as Glenpool Station), which was about 2.7 miles northeast of the Glenpool South tank farm, through a 12-inch-diameter ConocoPhillips pipeline.

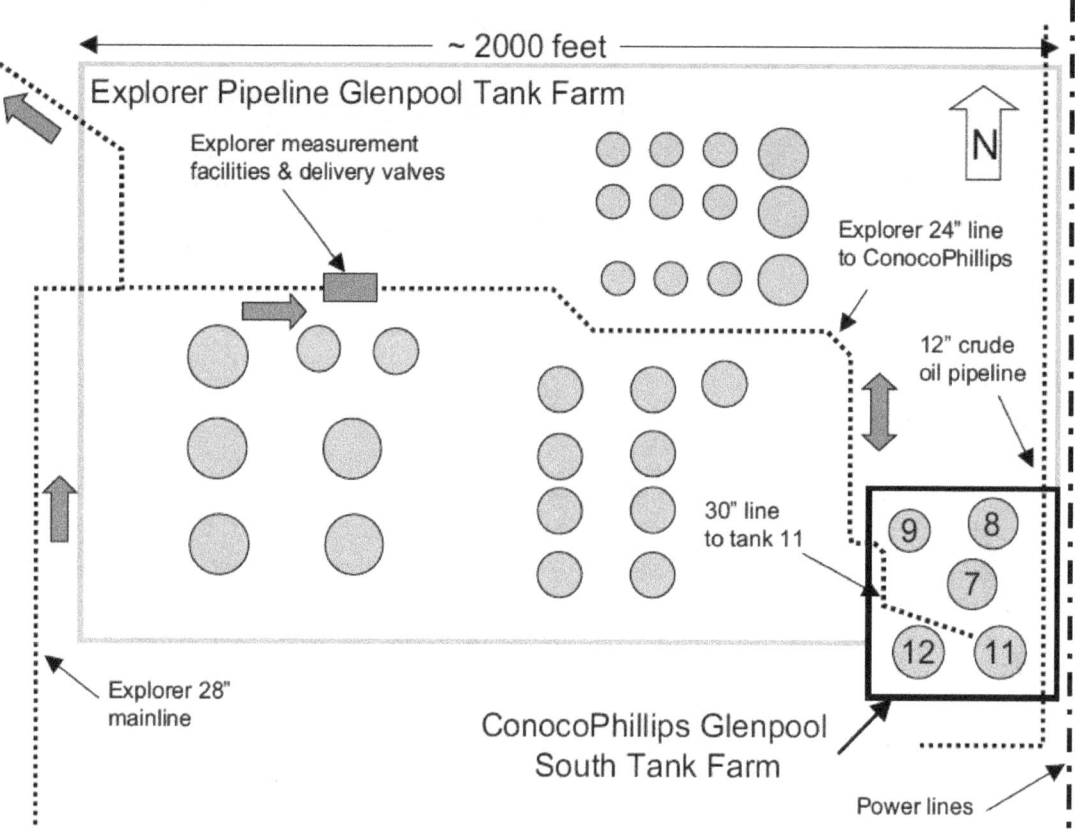

Figure 1. Schematic of Explorer Pipeline Glenpool tank farm and ConocoPhillips Glenpool South tank farm showing tank 11, pipelines, and power lines located along dike east of Glenpool South tank farm.

About 4:00 p.m. at Glenpool Terminal, the ConocoPhillips operator obtained a valve lineup sheet and prepared it jointly with the outgoing shift operator for the upcoming operations. Before leaving the office for the tank farm, the operator verified how much gasoline was in the piping system so that, once the removal operation was complete, she could confirm that all the gasoline had been removed. She went to the Glenpool South tank farm about 4:30 p.m. and began transferring gasoline from the manifold piping to tank 12. When the transfer of gasoline from tank 11 to Glenpool terminal was completed, about 5:33 p.m., she transferred the gasoline in the tank's piping to tank 12.

When all transfers were complete, about 6:10 p.m., the operator lined up the valves so tank 11 could receive diesel from Explorer. ConocoPhillips representatives told investigators that even though no gasoline remained in the tank 11 lines or manifold piping at the conclusion of the transfer operation, about 55 barrels of gasoline remained in the tank 11 sump[5] between the sump floor and the bottom of the 30-inch-diameter fill/drain pipe (which was about 21 inches above the sump floor).

About 6:15 p.m. on April 7, 2003, the ConocoPhillips operator went to the office at the Explorer Glenpool tank farm and spoke with the Explorer operator. The ConocoPhillips operator confirmed with the Explorer operator that the delivery was a 24,500-barrel batch of diesel going into tank 11, which was empty (except for the residual gasoline in the sump). The diesel delivery was from Explorer's 28-inch-diameter mainline. After the diesel was measured and sampled at the Explorer Glenpool facility, the delivery would continue through Explorer's 24-inch-diameter line to the ConocoPhillips 30-inch-diameter line and then into tank 11. The ConocoPhillips operator also confirmed that the maximum allowable fill amount was 75,079 barrels. The ConocoPhillips operator then opened two valves in Explorer's yard to line up the delivery; the delivery to ConocoPhillips commenced when Explorer control room personnel opened the delivery valve. Except for the opening of the delivery valve, lining up the valves, including the two valves in Explorer's yard, was the responsibility of the ConocoPhillips operator. About 6:30 p.m., after the valve lineup was completed, the ConocoPhillips operator returned to Glenpool Terminal.

About 8:33 p.m., Explorer switched the delivery of diesel to the line serving ConocoPhillips at an initial flow rate of 24,000 to 27,500 barrels per hour. The ConocoPhillips operator stated that at about 8:55 p.m., there was a high (product) level alarm in tank 11 and that this was odd because the delivery had just begun and tank 11 had been empty.

The Explorer operator at the Glenpool tank farm stated that he observed a fireball but that he was near operating pumps and did not hear an explosion. He described the accident as a flash, followed by smoke and fire, after which the fire totally engulfed tank 11. He said he went to his truck and drove to the Explorer control room, where he called the Explorer central control dispatcher. He said he then drove in his truck toward the fire to verify its location. It was determined that about 8:55 p.m., after tank 11 had been filling with diesel for about 22 minutes, the tank exploded. The fixed roof separated from the tank shell and was blown northward and folded over on itself, coming to rest on top of the collapsed north wall of the tank. (See figures 2 and 3.)

---

[5] The 15-foot-diameter by 6-foot-deep sump was in the northwest area of the tank floor, which sloped toward the sump. The design of tank 11 is discussed in more detail later in this report.

Figure 2. View of wreckage of tank 11 facing south. Note power lines and earthen dike at left and overpressure piping at right.

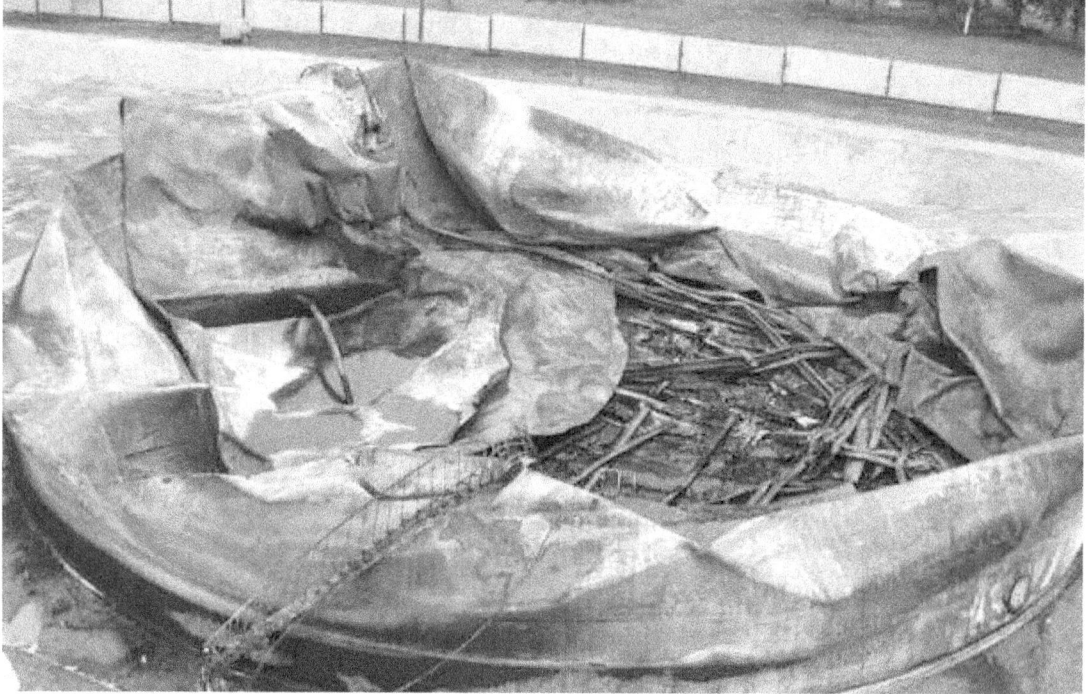

Figure 3. Wreckage of tank 11.

The Explorer operator then returned to the Explorer control room, and about 8:59 p.m. closed a valve to stop the diesel delivery to ConocoPhillips and switched the delivery to other tankage in the Explorer yard. At this time, the ConocoPhillips facility was isolated from Explorer's piping system. The Explorer operator called and informed the Explorer central control dispatcher that the delivery had been switched. He also called the operator at the ConocoPhillips Glenpool Terminal.

About this same time, the ConocoPhillips operator was calling the Explorer operator. The Explorer operator told the ConocoPhillips operator about the ball of fire, which they concluded was a tank on fire at the ConocoPhillips Glenpool South tank farm. The ConocoPhillips operator asked that the delivery be stopped. The two operators agreed that the Explorer operator would call 911 while the ConocoPhillips operator notified her supervisor.

After the Explorer operator called 911, he called his supervisor and asked that the supervisor contact Explorer central control and have controllers shut down the 28-inch pipeline that was supplying the diesel to the Explorer facility. Explorer shut down its 28-inch-diameter pipeline at Glenpool tank farm at about 9:35 p.m. and had all tank and header valves closed by about 9:45 p.m. Explorer's incident command was initially set up at 9:33 p.m. in the Glenpool tank farm control room and was moved to a conference room at 10:40 p.m.

A resident who was inside her house, about 1,000 feet east of tank 11, reported hearing a sound like thunder that rattled her house. She said she exited her house less than 30 seconds later, at which time there was a second explosion, this one with a higher pitched sound than the first. She observed that the north side of the tank had collapsed and was on fire and that the wind was blowing the flames south.

Power poles owned by American Electric Power (AEP)[6] were east of the tank farm over a wall on the dike that surrounded the tank farm. The electric power facilities included three conductor wires and two shield wires[7] supported by a single crossbar on dual wooden poles. Just before 6:00 a.m. on April 8, one or more wires on these poles fell to the ground. (See figure 4.) A fire then started in the unburned diesel that was being contained in the dike north of tank 11.

About 6:10 a.m. on April 8, 2003, crude oil at 550 pounds per square inch, gauge (psig) was released from aboveground piping between tanks 7 and 8 inside the dike after the piping was engulfed in fire started by the power lines. The piping system provided overpressure protection for ConocoPhillips' 12-inch-diameter crude oil pipeline. An isolation flange assembly in the piping failed because of the fire, allowing the pressurized crude oil to spray the surrounding area through the loosened flange assembly. By 6:17 a.m., ConocoPhillips had shut down the pipeline pumps and closed the remotely operated valves in the pipeline.

---

[6] AEP, which is based in Columbus, Ohio, operates an electricity transmission and distribution grid and is the Nation's largest electricity generator.

[7] A *shield wire* is a grounded conductor installed to shield a phase conductor from a direct lightning strike.

Figure 4. View of downed AEP power lines on east dike wall.

The ConocoPhillips Glenpool area supervisor initially estimated that about 7,400 barrels of diesel were in tank 11 at the time of the explosion. This figure was different from the 8,420 barrels read by Explorer's meter because some product was in the piping system downstream of the meter on its way to tank 11 when the explosion occurred.

Safety Board investigators calculated the amount of diesel that was in tank 11 at the time of the explosion. These calculations were based on the amount of gasoline that was in the tank 11 sump when delivery of diesel began, the quantity of diesel metered by Explorer during the delivery, the diesel that was metered after the explosion but that did not enter tank 11, and the quantity of diesel that remained in the previously empty delivery manifold and tank 11 piping at the time of the explosion. Based on these calculations, tank 11 contained between 7,397 and 7,600 barrels of liquid (diesel and a small amount of gasoline) at the time of the explosion.

Emergency Response

The Glenpool Fire Department received a 911 report of tank explosion and fire at 9:00 p.m. and was on scene by 9:06 p.m., at which time tank 11 had collapsed and was engulfed by flames 75 feet high.

The emergency response eventually involved 13 fire departments and firefighting personnel from ConocoPhillips, Sun Refinery, and Williams Fire and Hazard Control. ConocoPhillips had preplanned with Sun Refinery for mutual assistance in firefighting. Initially, the fire departments applied foam from the west side of the dike between tanks 7 and 12 and placed it around the burning tank so that the wind would disperse the foam to contain the ground fire. However, the manner in which the tank collapsed hindered the application of foam to the tank. Firefighters also applied water to tank 12, which contained gasoline, to cool it. Explorer and ConocoPhillips checked the dike drain valves to ensure that they were closed. After the power lines fell and diesel in the north area of the dike caught fire, a fire started inside tank 8 (which contained naphtha) in the area of the internal floating roof seal. This fire eventually extinguished itself, and the heat from the internal fire damaged tank 8. Also, the burning diesel in the north area of the dike caused a flange assembly in the crude oil pipeline overpressure protection system to fail and release crude oil in the area.

The ConocoPhillips Glenpool area supervisor stated that because of a concern about the quantity of foam available, he called ConocoPhillips in Ponca City for additional supplies. Another ConocoPhillips employee called the Sinclair Refinery and the Tulsa airport and asked for information about available foam supplies. A staging area was set up to receive foam deliveries.

In addition to a family living approximately 1,000 feet east of the tank farm, about 300 families living near the tank farm were evacuated. This was a voluntary evacuation that was lifted on the afternoon of April 9. ConocoPhillips provided housing for the evacuees. Nearby schools were closed for 2 days.

Several AEP employees called the AEP transmission system operator between 9:00 p.m. and 9:30 p.m. to notify him of the accident, but he had already seen the fire on the television news. He stated that he knew the AEP power lines were near the fire.

About midnight, ConocoPhillips personnel called the AEP dispatcher and requested that an AEP representative inspect the power lines near and to the east of the tank, because the flames were impinging on them. At 12:30 a.m. on April 8, an AEP servicer was dispatched to the site, and by 1:14 a.m., he had inspected the power lines and reported to the transmission system operator. No sag in the lines was observed, and the servicer, who did not communicate with any incident command staff, returned home. He did suggest to the AEP transmission system operator that an AEP representative inspect the wooden power pole near the fire, but there is no record of action being taken.

About 3:43 a.m., the incident command noted that the wind had shifted to the east, but the tank 11 fire appeared contained, the cooling operation on tanks 7 and 12 was successful, and the incident appeared to be stable. Within an hour, however, the fire in tank 11 was worse, possibly because the firefighting foam inside the tank was degrading.

About 5:00 a.m., after having been contacted again by on-scene personnel at 4:45 a.m., the AEP dispatcher again called the servicer at home. The transmission system operator documented in his log that the fire had restarted and was worse than before and that AEP should recheck the lines. The servicer returned to the scene at about 5:30 a.m. and observed that the conductor closest to the fire now had a slight sag. This indicated that heat from the fire was affecting the power line. Incident command was notified that the servicer was on site, but the servicer did not check in or otherwise communicate with incident command. About 20 minutes later, one or more wires fell onto the diked area east of the tanks and the diesel that was contained inside that area of the dike ignited.

The AEP transmission system operator stated that any decision to deenergize the lines was to be made by him based on information provided by the on-site inspectors and an AEP field representative. He stated that if these lines had been deenergized, power would have been cut to the AEP substation at an Explorer pump station (not at the Glenpool tank farm) and to the pump station. No other outages would have been expected, because the system would have automatically rerouted power.

The AEP transmission system operator stated that his emergency response training had not included training for nonelectrical issues. He said his training had involved neither visits to the ConocoPhillips Glenpool South tank farm nor face-to-face meetings with ConocoPhillips personnel. The AEP field representative stated that his training had been primarily on the job and that he had gained experience in actual emergencies.

Meteorological Information

No lightning was reported or noted in the area at the time of the explosion. The temperature was about 52° F, and the relative humidity was 54 percent. The wind was from the north at 7 mph gusting to 16 mph.

ConocoPhillips Glenpool Facilities

The ConocoPhillips[8] Glenpool South tank farm, constructed between 1978 and 1981, was originally a Conoco facility and consisted of four storage tanks, which were designated 7, 8, 11, and 12, and one smaller tank, designated 9, that was used for mixed products. The tanks were inside a dike consisting of earthen walls and a crushed rock surface. Outside the dike were a control building, valve manifolds, product pumps, a vacuum pump and tank, and an underground sump connected to the vacuum tank.

Except for tank 9, the tanks had a "drain dry" design. The floor of tank 11 was sloped to a sump inside the tank, and the 30-inch-diameter common fill/drain piping terminated in the sump. When the tank was drained dry, the only liquid that remained in the tank was approximately 55 barrels in the sump below the bottom of the fill/drain piping.

---

[8] ConocoPhillips was founded in 2002 when Conoco, Inc., and Phillips Petroleum Company merged.

Tank 11 and Appurtenances

ConocoPhillips representatives told investigators that no as-built design or construction drawings for tank 11 could be found. According to ConocoPhillips, tanks 11 and 12 were both constructed in 1981 and were similar in design and construction.

The following information was obtained from the tank nameplates, the inspection report from the tank 11 external inspection performed in July 2000, the construction specification for tanks 11 and 12, a ConocoPhillips as-built drawing of the tank 11 and tank 12 sump, and photographic evidence and known data from tank 12.[9] Tank 11 was a 48-foot-high by 109-foot-diameter welded steel storage tank with a cone-type fixed roof and an internal floating roof (see figure 5). The purpose of a floating roof is to minimize emissions and evaporative losses. It floated on pontoons on top of the product and was equipped with legs that supported the roof when product was drained from the tank and the volume of liquid in the tank decreased to the level at which the roof no longer floated. The ability to "land" the roof, meaning that the roof was sitting on and fully supported by the legs, also prevented it from being damaged by contacting the tank floor. The legs typically are set so the roof is about 3 feet above the tank floor but they can be set at approximately 6 feet to facilitate personnel entering the tank and working under the roof.

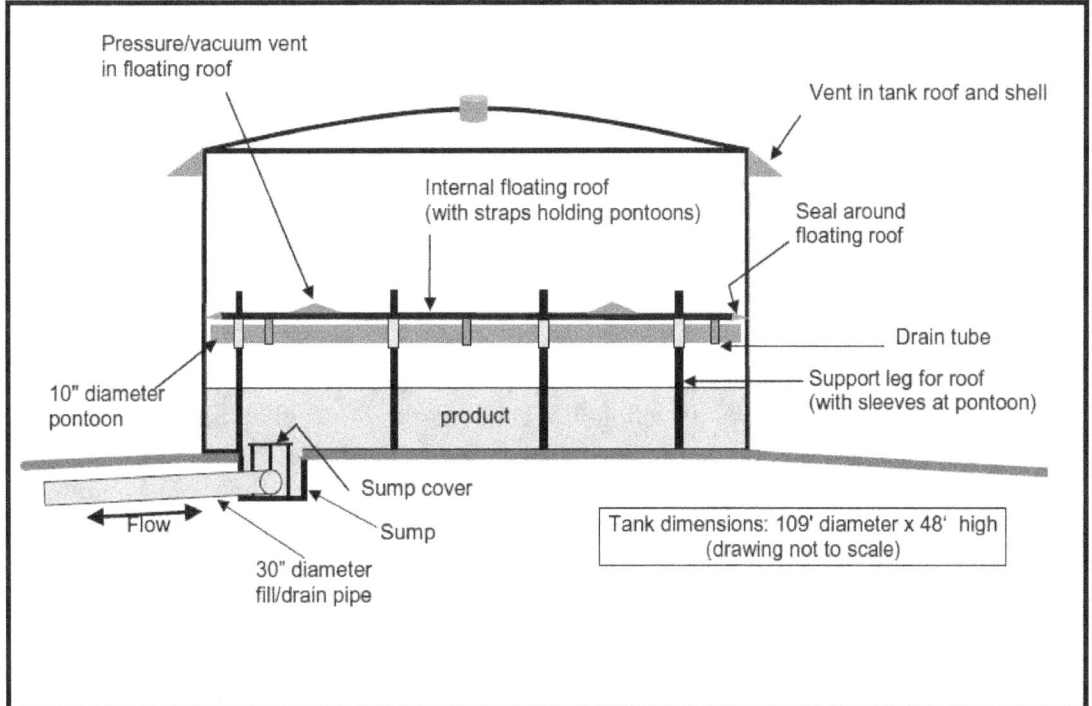

Figure 5. Diagram of storage tank showing floating roof and sump.

---

[9] Investigators were able to internally inspect tank 12, which was out of service for maintenance after the accident.

Continental Pipe Line Company (predecessor of ConocoPhillips) had specified that tank 11 be designed and constructed by Webco Tank, Inc., in accordance with American Petroleum Institute (API) Standard 650 (*Welded Steel Tanks for Oil Storage),* Appendices D, G, and K. Continental Pipe Line Company had specified that the tank be designed for a range of refined products, including gasoline and diesel, and have a nominal capacity of 80,000 barrels. The design pressure was 4 to 14 psig. The maximum design fill rate was specified to be 32,000 barrels per hour, and the maximum design flow rate for emptying the tank was specified to be 20,000 barrels per hour. Data regarding the design basis for the maximum fill and empty rates were not available.

The tank shell was supported on a concrete ring wall foundation. Four ground lugs around the perimeter of the tank were used to ground the tank. There were nine vent openings in the shell near the top of tank and six vents in the fixed roof. The tank floor sloped to a 15-foot-diameter by 6-foot-deep steel sump. The tank did not have a mixer. The datum plate[10] was mounted on the south wall of the tank.

A 24- and 30-inch-diameter fill/drain pipe connected the manifold piping to the sump. A 30-inch-diameter tee was welded to the end of the 30-inch-diameter pipe inside the sump, which was about 9 feet from the tank wall. A 6-foot by 12-foot rectangular splash plate covered the sump about 6 inches above the tank floor. (The diagrams in figure 6 show the configuration of the sump in tank 11.)

The floating roof assembly was fabricated and installed by Altech Industries in 1981. Baker Tank Company (which acquired Altech Industries, Inc., in the mid-1980s) stated that the floating roofs in tanks 11 and 12 were of the same design, materials, and construction. The assembly was aluminum and consisted of a flat roof deck mounted on 10-inch diameter horizontal pontoons. The pontoons were designed to provide sufficient buoyancy to prevent the roof deck from contacting the product in the tank. Spaced throughout the area of the floating roof were aluminum drain tubes. Rows of "C" channels were attached to the sheet metal that formed the deck to provide stiffness. The design documents also showed two "pressure/vacuum vents/manway" openings in the floating roof deck. A butyl nitrile wiper seal around the perimeter of the floating roof was intended to act as a vapor seal to reduce the amount of vapor lost to the environment when the tank contained high-volatile hydrocarbon liquids. The wiper seal in tank 11 was installed in 1995 as a replacement for the original Midwest Urethane Waffle Wiper seal. During the inspection of tank 12, the floating roof was supported on legs that placed it about 6 feet above the floor. Investigators noted that the roof was not centered in the tank while it sat on the legs and that a gap large enough to insert a closed fist existed between the tank wall and the flexible seal attached to the floating roof on one side of the roof. On the opposite side from this gap, the flexible seal was compressed tightly against the interior tank wall.

---

[10] A *datum plate* is a level metal plate mounted near the floor of a storage tank that is used for measuring the depth of liquid in the tank. The depth is measured using a tape lowered through an opening in the tank's roof to the datum plate. The volume of liquid in the tank can then be determined by looking up the depth measurement on a strapping table. A *strapping table* shows for the height (level) of product in a tank the volume (quantity) of product in the tank.

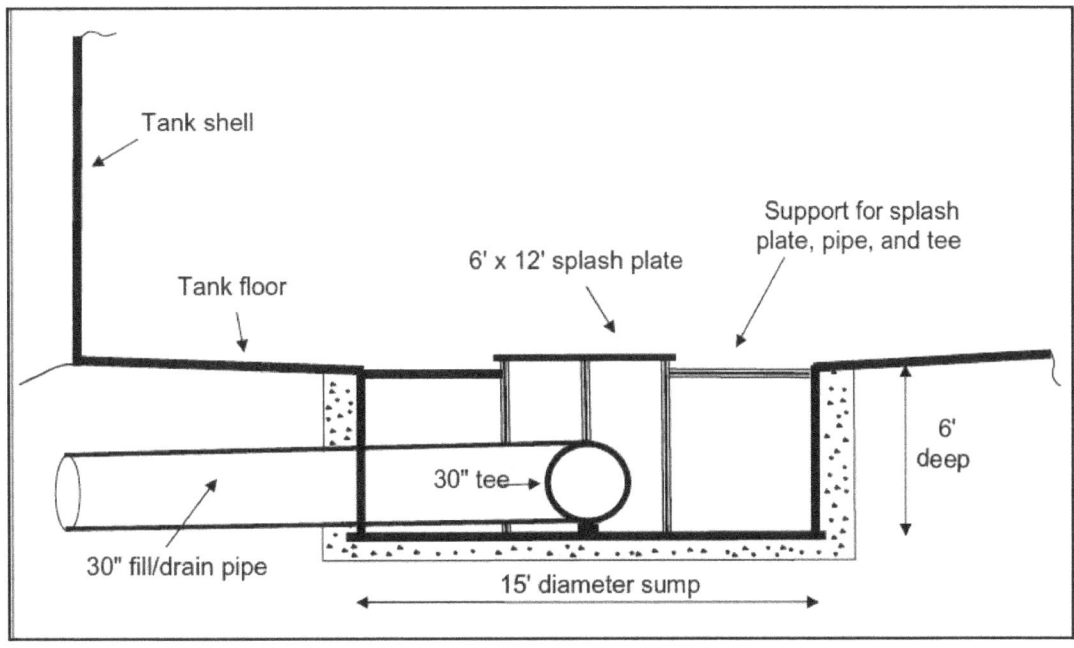

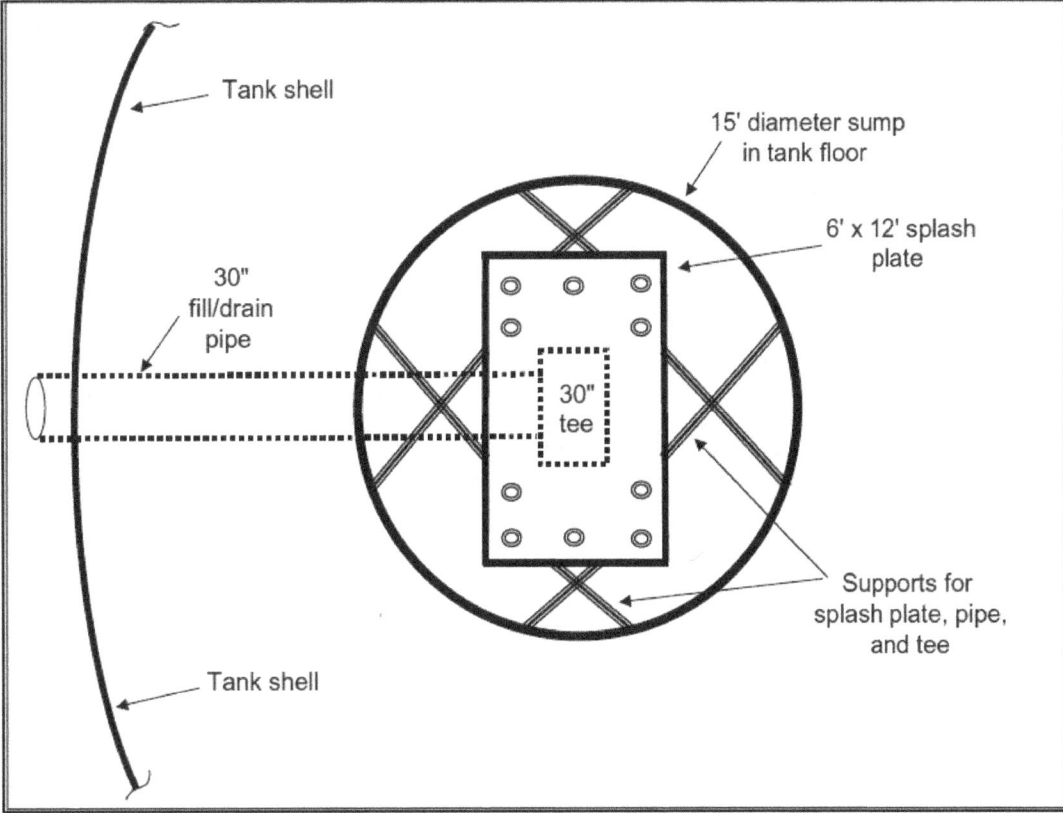

Figure 6. Tank 11 sump and fill/drain piping viewed from the side (top diagram) and from above (bottom diagram).

The legs of the floating roof were fitted through aluminum sleeves fastened to the floating roof. The legs could be adjusted to support the roof at different heights above the tank floor when the roof was not floating. Leg length was determined by placing bolts with nuts through predrilled holes in the sleeve and leg above the roof. A bolt and nut could also be placed in the leg below the floating roof to prevent it from descending all the way to the tank floor. Thirty-four legs extended around the interior circumference of the tank, approximately 4 inches inside the tank wall. The interior portion of the roof had about 14 more legs. The strapping table provided to investigators indicated that 7,180 barrels of product would be required to fully float the roof, and that product would first contact the pontoons at a volume of 6,390 barrels. Steel columns that supported the fixed roof extended from the tank floor through the floating roof to the fixed roof. Antirotation cables for the floating roof were installed. The roof had drains approximately 11 inches long. In tank 12, investigators observed that one drain tube was longer than the others and extended below the bottom of the nearby pontoon. (See figure 7.)

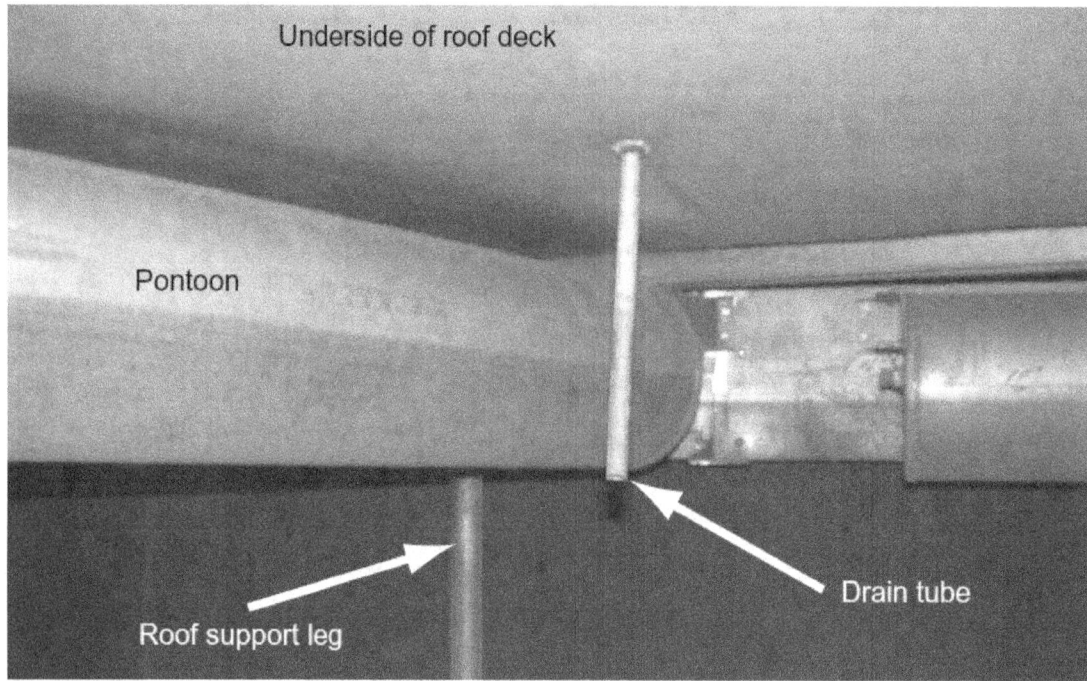

Figure 7. Drain tube extending down from floating roof in tank 12.

The floating roof bonding system for tank 11 consisted of stainless steel wires that connected the floating roof to the fixed roof. The purpose of the wires was to keep the floating roof and the tank roof/shell at the same electrical potential for protection against electrostatic discharges.[11] At the fixed roof, according to the roof drawings, one pair of wires was connected to each of two eyebolts. Each pair of wires was connected to the eyebolt by a knot through the eye of the bolt for strain relief. In addition, a loop of the wire was mechanically clamped to an aluminum grounding clip, which was bolted to the shank

---

[11] Bond wires connect two conductors (in this case the floating roof and the fixed roof) so they are at the same electrical potential.

of the eyebolt on the inside of the fixed roof. At the floating roof, each of the four wires was screwed to the frame of the roof in several places.

Baker Tank Company provided a data sheet that documented the construction inspection and the as-installed condition of tank 11's floating roof. This document indicates that the distance from the tank floor (measured adjacent to the manual gauge funnel near the tank wall) to the underside of the roof deck panels was 62 3/8 inches. The data sheet also documented that the installation of the bond wires at both the fixed roof and the floating roof had been checked.

The strapping table provided to investigators indicated that at a volume of approximately 7,180 barrels (3 feet 6 inches above the datum plate) the roof was fully floating, and at a volume of approximately 6,390 barrels (3 feet above the datum plate), liquid in the tank first contacted the roof pontoons.

Two alarms were set in the supervisory control and data acquisition system (SCADA)[12] to alert the controllers when the volume in the tank was nearing the level at which the roof would no longer float. The set points for the alarms were based on the landed height of the floating roof assumed in the ConocoPhillips strapping table. Based on the measurement of the height of the floating roof documented on the construction inspection report and based on measurements investigators made of the tank 11 legs and the floating roof in tank 12, the strapping table was determined to be incorrect. Investigators determined that the distance from the bottom of a pontoon to the datum plate while the tank 11 roof was landed was between 3 feet 8 inches and 3 feet 9 inches. Based on this information, investigators prepared a revised strapping table. From the revised table, it was determined that liquid in tank 11 would first contact the floating roof when the volume was between approximately 7,498 and 7,632 barrels.

Tank Farm

West of the tank farm and outside of the diked area, two pipelines to/from Explorer's facility—a 24-inch-diameter and a 30-inch-diameter—and the ConocoPhillips 12-inch-diameter pipeline to/from Glenpool Terminal were connected to manifolds. The manifolds were an interconnection of pipe and valves that, through the opening and closing of selected valves, allowed product to flow into or out of individual tanks as needed. These valves were either manually or motor operated, and none of them could be remotely operated. ConocoPhillips had no equipment at this facility to control the flow rate to its tank 11 from Explorer. For product movements to Glenpool Terminal in the 12-inch-diameter pipeline, a ConocoPhillips pump was used, or the product was transferred by gravity. For product transfers to Explorer, the 30-inch-diameter line gravity fed product into a pump in Explorer's yard.

---

[12] Pipeline system controllers use SCADA systems to remotely monitor and control movement of liquids in pipelines and related facilities, such as tank farms. With a SCADA system, controllers can monitor operating parameters—such as tank volumes, product flow rates, pressures, temperatures, valve status, and alarms—and control valves and pumps to adjust the flow in the pipeline system.

The manifold area also included vacuum system equipment. The vacuum process was intended to minimize the mixing of incompatible products, such as gasoline and diesel, when the same piping was used to transport different products. The system consisted of a vacuum pump, vacuum tank, storage sump, sump pump, and interconnecting piping. The system functioned to remove product from three areas: the manifold piping, the piping connecting the manifolds to the individual storage tanks, and the tank sump above the bottom of the fill/drain piping. The vacuumed product was collected in a vacuum tank and drained by gravity into a storage sump before being either pumped to a storage tank suitable for the product or otherwise disposed of. The ConocoPhillips Glenpool South Station log documents that the volume of the 24-inch manifold header was 49 barrels, and the volume of the tank 11 fill/drain piping was 253 barrels.

Additional piping unrelated to the storage tanks was inside the diked area east of tank 7. This aboveground pipe and valves included a rupture disk and isolation flange. The rupture disk provided overpressure protection for a ConocoPhillips 12-inch-diameter crude oil pipeline—designated the Wood River crude oil pipeline—that was underground along the east side of the dike. In the event of a pipeline overpressure, the rupture disk would break and relieve the pressure in the pipeline by directing the crude oil into tank 9. The isolation flange assembly included a nonmetallic gasket and was part of the cathodic protection system for the pipeline. The isolation flange assembly electrically insulated the crude oil pipeline from the tank farm facilities.

Inside the diked area were several light poles and electrical junction boxes. The junction box between tanks 11 and 12 was an explosion-proof enclosure. Inside this box was wiring for controls and instruments, such as tank level gauges and motor-operated valve controls, which was connected to terminal strips.

ConocoPhillips representatives told investigators that there were no security cameras at the Glenpool South tank farm and that the site was secured with a chain link fence and locked gate. The ConocoPhillips operator on duty stated that this gate was closed and locked when she arrived at the Glenpool South tank farm about 4:30 p.m. on April 7, 2003.

Control Centers

ConocoPhillips had a local control center at Glenpool Terminal and a control panel at Glenpool South tank farm that was connected to the local control center. The control computer polled the station sensors about once a second. The status of each valve and pump was recorded if it had changed from the previous polling. Other data included readings from instruments for temperature, pressure, and product gravity. The tank 11 level gauge data was not received in the local control center at Glenpool Terminal because some of the level gauge data lines had been disconnected in preparation for the installation of a new radar level gauge. However, tank 11 level data was still being transmitted to, monitored at, and recorded at the ConocoPhillips central control center at Ponca City, about 80 miles northwest of the Glenpool South tank farm. This control center had a SCADA system that operated ConocoPhillips pipelines via satellite links and that monitored some of the valves, pumps, and sensors at Glenpool South tank farm. The

ConocoPhillips system was set up so that the operator at Glenpool Terminal controlled the local operations while the controller in Ponca City monitored the station activities and coordinated operations when product flowed into, or out of, the Glenpool stations.

The height of product in tank 11 was measured with a level gauge that transmitted the data to the Ponca City control system via a satellite link. The control system computer converted the height data into tank volume using strapping table measurements and other corrections. The tank level was sampled every minute, and the level was recorded if it had changed from the previous reading. The timestamp on the data indicated when the SCADA system received the data. Because of polling and transmission times, delays of up to 1.5 minutes could occur between the time an event occurred and the time it was recorded.

Explorer Glenpool Facilities

Explorer Pipeline Company's Glenpool tank farm consisted of 31 tanks, which had a combined capacity of about 3.4 million barrels, and it was adjacent to and northwest of the ConocoPhillips Glenpool South tank farm. Except for a backpressure regulator that maintained a constant pressure at Explorer's meter, equipment at Explorer's Glenpool tank farm did not control the flow rate to tankage at the ConocoPhillips Glenpool South tank farm.

Data from the Glenpool tank farm flow computer and valves, pumps, and sensors were transmitted via local telephone lines to Explorer's central control center in Tulsa, Oklahoma. Sensors were polled about every 5 seconds, and the data were recorded in a SCADA system.

American Electric Power Equipment

Power poles owned by AEP were east of the tank farm on top of the dike wall. The facilities included three conductors rated at 138,000 volts and two shield wires. This power line was originally built in 1930–1931 as a 66,000-volt line and was rebuilt in the same location in 1950 as a 138,000-volt line. After the accident, AEP replaced one set of wooden poles on the dike wall near tanks 7 and 11 with a single steel pole, which raised the wires in this area.

Postaccident Field Inspections

Tank 11 Wreckage

The floating roof and appurtenances had been severely damaged by the explosion, by heat from the fire, and by the collapse of the fixed roof and tank walls. Eleven floating roof legs were recovered from the debris of the burned tank. Pieces of four legs below the sleeves were recovered and reassembled. The recovered sleeves were observed to be resting on a bolt and nut assembly through the legs, which was between 51 1/2 and 52 inches above the leg foot that rested on the floor of the tank near the tank wall. Based on these measurements, the distance from the datum plate (which was 6 3/4 inches above the tank floor in tank 12) to the bottom of a floating roof pontoon was about 3 feet 8 inches. This was about 8 inches higher than indicated on the original strapping table and, based on a corrected strapping table prepared by investigators, is equivalent to a product volume of between 7,498 and 7,632 barrels.

Pontoons that were recovered were discolored; examination of the discoloration indicated that when the roof was floating about 5 inches of the pontoons were submerged. Several roof drain tubes were recovered. The tubes appeared to be made of aluminum and were approximately 11 inches long and 1/2 inch in diameter. The lower 5 inches of the recovered tubes were discolored.

On-site examination of tank 11 revealed that two eyebolts were attached to the fixed roof. The eyebolt that was recovered from the folded-over portion of the fixed roof outside the tank on the north side was designated eyebolt No. 1, and the eyebolt that was recovered in the northeast area of the wreckage on the tank floor was designated eyebolt No. 2. A portion of the threaded shank of each eyebolt was found inserted into a hole in the fixed roof. The surfaces of all the eyebolts and wire cables were covered with black soot, consistent with exposure to fire. The disassembled eyebolts and wire cables were sent to the Safety Board Materials Laboratory for examination.

Examination of eyebolt No. 2 revealed that a wire cable was tied to the curved head portion. A looped portion of the same wire cable extended beyond the tied knot on the curved head. Solidified metal was found next to the eyebolt. The solidified metal encased a steel bolt and a portion of the looped end of the wire cable. The looped end of the wire cable was wrapped around the bolt. A nut and washer were found attached to the threaded shank portion of the eyebolt. Solidified metal also was found between the nut and the washer.

A wire cable was tied to the curved head portion of eyebolt No. 1 similar to eyebolt No. 2. The looped end of the wire cable that extended from the tied knot had been deformed and was flat. The threaded shank portion of eyebolt No. 1 in two areas was covered with solidified metal.

The eyebolts were pulled from the wall of the fixed roof by hand without effort. During handling of eyebolt No. 2, the solidified metal fragment separated from the looped end of the wire cable. The looped end of the wire also fractured during this separation event. Two of the four locations where the bond wires were connected at the floating roof were discovered in the wreckage. At these locations, the bond wires were connected to the floating roof structure with screws.

ConocoPhillips Crude Oil Pipeline

The aboveground piping associated with the ConocoPhillips crude oil pipeline overpressure protection was in the pool of burning diesel. The pipe and valves were burned, but they did not appear to have ruptured. The cathodic protection isolation flange assembly was on the pipeline side of the first aboveground valve. Crude oil was observed in a drip pan that had been placed below the flange. Black discoloration was observed on the west side of approximately seven of the concrete fence panels adjacent to the crude piping. This fence appeared to delineate the tank farm area from the adjacent property. Some crude oil had sprayed over the fence onto the ground.

AEP Power Lines

On April 10, 2003, investigators observed the power lines and shield wires on the ground on the east wall of the Glenpool South tank farm dike. The wooden power poles were standing.

ConocoPhillips Electrical Facilities

At the time of the accident, a radar gauging system for the tanks at Glenpool South tank farm was being installed. For this gauging system, new electrical conduit had been run from the tops of the tanks into the common explosion-proof electrical junction box between tanks 11 and 12. No wiring had been installed in the new conduits, although they were connected to the junction box. The existing conduit/electrical wiring to this box had vapor seals where it entered the electrical box. No vapor seals were observed in the new conduit for the radar gauging system. This conduit was also open to the atmosphere at the top of the tank, in some cases near the tank roof vents.

Because the conduit was open from the junction box to the tops of tanks 11 and 12, this conduit was considered a potential path for flammable vapors to enter the junction box. It was hypothesized that flammable vapors from a tank could have been drawn into the open conduit due to strong winds at the time of the explosion and ignited. The flame front could then have traveled back to the vent opening in tank 11, igniting the vapors in the tank. Consequently, before the junction box was opened for examination, a water manometer was attached to the conduit where it entered the electrical box, and the other end of the manometer was open to the atmosphere. The purpose of this measurement was to determine whether a pressure differential (chimney effect) existed between the electrical box and the atmosphere. No pressure differential was noted.

When the electrical box was opened and examined, discoloration was found on the bottom of a hole where the new conduit from the new gauge on tank 11 entered the electrical box. However, no evidence of an electric arc was observed in the junction box.

The new conduit to tank 11 was excavated to examine the inside of the conduit for soot or other evidence of fire inside the conduit. After the conduit was exposed and opened, it was observed that it was filled with clear water. The installer stated that the conduit was not designed to be watertight.

Tests and Research

Safety Board Materials Laboratory Examination

Detailed laboratory examination of the two eyebolts and the wires to which they were attached revealed no evidence of arc-related pitting damage, discoloration, or deposits that can result from electrical discharge. The fractured ends of the wires from each cable exhibited elongation deformation and knife edges that are typical of overstress separation. The eyebolts and wire showed no evidence of a preexisting crack or corrosion.

The eyebolt threads were covered with deposits of aluminum, indicating that an aluminum grounding clip and aluminum nuts had melted during the fire. The wire found at eyebolt No. 2 was looped around a steel bolt and embedded in solidified metal, which was determined to be melted aluminum. The wire in the general location of the bolt showed evidence of flattening, which was consistent with the wire having been connected to the aluminum grounding clip with a nut and bolt. A coating found on both eyebolts was determined to consist of uniform layers of iron oxide, which is typical of oxidation that occurs rapidly at elevated temperatures.

Diesel Analysis

The diesel delivered to tank 11 on April 7 originated at a refinery near Pasadena, Texas, and had been stored in a tank there. The refinery arranged for samples to be taken from the tank. An independent lab working for the refinery prepared a "Certificate of Analysis" for these samples, which were referred to as "low sulfur diesel."

A sample of the diesel being delivered to ConocoPhillips tank 11 was taken by Explorer at its Glenpool tank farm approximately 5,000 barrels into the delivery. Explorer's procedures required that a sample be drawn from the beginning, middle, and end of the batch; however, because the scheduled 24,500-barrel delivery of diesel ended after approximately 8,420 barrels, it was not possible to draw a sample from the middle and the end of the batch.

The Safety Board had a portion of Explorer's sample tested by an independent laboratory. No samples of diesel were collected after the fire because the firefighting efforts had contaminated the diesel with water and other products. The following tests were conducted:

- Flash point,[13] according to American Society for Testing and Materials (ASTM) D-93, Standard Test Methods for Flash-Point by Pensky-Martens Closed Cup Tester.

- Distillation curve, according to ASTM D-86, Standard Test Method for Distillation of Petroleum Products at Atmospheric Pressure.

---

[13] *Flash point* is the lowest temperature at which a liquid releases enough vapors to the air to form an ignitable mixture. The flash point of gasoline is approximately -50° F.

- Electrical conductivity, according to ASTM D-2624, Standard Test Methods for Electrical Conductivity of Aviation and Distillate Fuels.

- Water content, according to ASTM D-1744, Standard Test Method for Determination of Water in Liquid Petroleum Products by Karl Fischer Reagent.

The flash point of the diesel was 162° F; the distillation curve showed it to be a "typical" diesel; the electrical conductivity was less than 1 pS/m;[14] the water content was 65 parts per million by weight.

Design Criteria for Tank Fill Rate

ConocoPhillips representatives told investigators that they had no documentation explaining how the maximum fill rate of 32,000 barrels per hour in the fill/drain pipe for tank 11 had been determined. They noted that the company's current design procedures were based on API Recommended Practice (RP) 2003, *Protection Against Ignitions Arising Out of Static, Lightning, and Stray Currents*.

Switch Loading

ConocoPhillips had previously conducted switch loading operations in tank 11 without incident. "Switch loading" refers to filling a tank, which previously contained a high- or intermediate-vapor-pressure product, with a low-vapor-pressure product.[15] ("Vapor pressure" is the pressure exerted by a gas in equilibrium with a liquid at a given temperature. High-vapor-pressure products include aviation gasoline, motor gasoline, and naphtha. Intermediate-vapor-pressure products include toluene, xylene, benzene, and jet fuel [JP-4, Jet B]. Low-vapor-pressure products include heating oil, kerosene, diesel, and safety solvents.)

At normal ambient temperatures, when a tank is filled with a high-vapor-pressure product, such as gasoline, the vapor space above the surface of the liquid becomes too rich to be flammable. When a tank is being filled with a low-vapor-pressure product, such as diesel, and there are no residual vapors in the tank, the vapor pressure of the diesel is too low to make the vapor-air mixture above the surface of the liquid flammable unless the ambient temperature is at or above the flash point of the product. For the accident switch load, the diesel temperature (66° F) and the ambient temperature (52° F) were well below the flash point of the diesel (162° F).

---

[14] Electrical conductivity is a measure of how well a material accommodates the transport of an electric charge, which is the movement of charged particles through a material in response to an electric field. The unit of measurement is Siemens/meter, or S/m. The prefix "p" is "pico" and equals 1 trillionth, or 10^{-12}. The conductivity of typical diesel is 0.5 to 50 pS/m.

[15] Other operations in which a tank is filled with a product different from its previous contents, including filling a tank with a product that has a vapor pressure higher than the vapor pressure of the product previously in the tank, do not pose the hazards associated with switch loading, and are not called switch loading.

For combustion to occur in air with a hydrocarbon fuel, two conditions must be met: an ignition source must be present, and the fuel vapor concentration must be between the lower and upper flammability limits for that particular hydrocarbon vapor. Outside this range, the vapor-air mixture is either too lean or too rich to be ignited. The flammability is dependent on the liquid's vapor pressure and the environment in which it is handled.

At the time of the accident, a switch loading operation was being conducted by loading diesel into a tank that had previously contained gasoline. Because of the hazards involved in this type of operation, both the National Fire Protection Association (NFPA) and the API have specific guidelines for dealing with the switching of product in a tank.[16] Both organizations recommend precautions if the vapor space in a tank is at or above the lower flammable limit because of the previously stored product and if the tank is to be filled with a low-vapor-pressure, low-conductivity (static accumulating) product. These precautions include minimizing static generation, preventing charge accumulation, avoiding spark discharge, and controlling the environment inside the tank.

Specific recommendations are suggested to minimize generation of static charge; these include avoiding splash filling and upward spraying, limiting the initial fill line and discharge velocities, avoiding loose or floating ungrounded conductive objects (such as gauge floats or sample cans) in the tank, avoiding pumping or flowing hydrocarbons with dispersed water or solids, and limiting the maximum fill rate. For floating roof tanks, these precautions apply until the roof is floating, after which the liquid surface is at the same electrical potential as the floating roof, and the vapor space has been reduced.

Factors that contribute to generating a flammable environment include the types of products involved, the amount of time the floating roof is landed with product in the tank, and the time the tank has for ventilation.

Switch Loading and Tank 11 Operations

Investigators reviewed switch loading records from January 2002 to the time of the accident to determine whether there were any differences in the conditions of these switch loading operations. Three previous switch loading operations were noted during this period.

Before each of these switch loading operations, the floating roof landed as the high-vapor-pressure product drained from the tank. Draining operations continued until the tank was empty (except for the approximately 55 barrels of liquid in the sump) and remained empty until the switch load (refilling the tank with low-vapor-pressure product) occurred. In the accident switch load, the floating roof landed as the gasoline drained from the tank on April 4. However, the draining operation was terminated before the tank was empty. On April 5, 1,897 barrels of gasoline were transferred from tank 10 to tank 11 with the intent of refloating the roof. The next day, an additional 1,819 barrels of gasoline were

---

[16] NFPA 30: *Flammable and Combustible Liquids Code;* NFPA 77: *Recommended Practice on Static Electricity;* API Recommended Practice 2003: *Protection Against Ignitions Arising out of Static, Lightning, and Stray Currents.*

added to the tank. (This gasoline was displaced from a pipeline connecting to the Glenpool South tank farm when naphtha was delivered in this pipeline to tank 8.) Based on the corrected strapping table, the tank 11 roof was not floating until this gasoline was added on April 6. The switch load occurred on April 7. The graph in figure 8 illustrates the volume in tank 11 from the morning of April 4, 2004, through the time of the accident on April 7. It is based on data from the tank 11 level gauge.

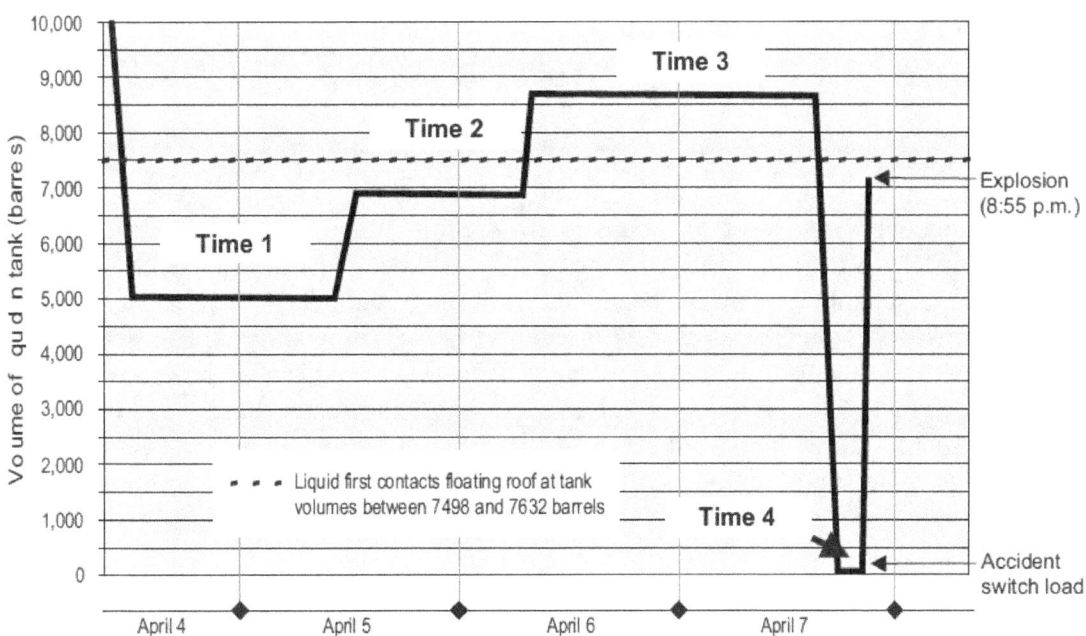

Figure 8. Volume of fuels in tank 11 during the 84 hours before the accident.

Safety Board Vapor Concentration Study

The Safety Board performed a study of vapor concentration to determine whether the environment in tank 11 was flammable at various times during tank operations on April 4 through April 7. Calculations of the fuel vapor concentration within tank 11 were made for four time periods of interest; they are shown in figure 8. At each time period, vapor concentrations were calculated for the spaces above and below the floating roof. The results of these calculations are shown in table 1.

Table 1. Volume concentration of gasoline vapor above and below the floating roof.

	Above the Roof (%)	Below the Roof (%)
Time 1	0	44–54
Time 2	1.2–1.4	44–54
Time 3	1.5–1.9	44–54*
Time 4	1.3–1.6	1.9–2.3

* The roof assembly was floating with the pontoons in contact with the gasoline during this period. The underside of the internal floating roof deck was approximately 7 inches above the surface of the liquid.

ConocoPhillips operating records show that after removal of gasoline from the tank on April 4, the tank still held 4,994 barrels of gasoline, which was insufficient to float the roof. This amount of gasoline remained in the tank until 8:00 a.m. on April 5 (the period shown as "Time 1" on table 1). Landing the roof allowed gasoline vapors to be produced in the space between the liquid and the floating roof. Calculations show that the vapor space would have become too rich to support combustion because the elapsed time was sufficient to allow the gasoline vapors to reach equilibrium. There would not have been any gasoline vapors introduced to the area between the fixed roof and the floating roof at this time.

The 8:00 a.m. delivery on April 5 introduced another 1,897 barrels of gasoline into the tank, bringing the total amount in the tank to 6,891 barrels, which was still insufficient to float the roof. The gasoline entering the tank displaced some of the vapor that had collected below the floating roof. This vapor moved up through the two vents in the floating roof and collected in the space between the fixed roof and the floating roof. The vapor concentration below the floating roof was calculated to be still too rich to support combustion. The vapor concentration above the roof was calculated to be within the flammable range.

This amount of gasoline in the tank remained at 6,891 barrels until 3:00 a.m. on April 6 ("Time 2" on table 1), when another 1,819 barrels were added. During this delivery, at about 3:30 a.m., the liquid level reached the pontoons of the floating roof, and the roof began to float. At the end of this delivery, tank 11 held 8,710 barrels of gasoline. At this time, calculations indicate that the space between the fixed roof and the floating roof was still within the flammable range even with the addition of vapors from below. The roof remained floating for another 36 hours ("Time 3") until the gasoline in the tank was pumped to other tankage.

The tank was then drained dry (except for the sump) and remained this way for 3 hours ("Time 4"). While the tank was draining, the roof landed, and some of the vapor that had collected between the fixed roof and the floating roof was transferred back below the floating roof. At this time in the operation, calculations show that a flammable environment existed both below and above the floating roof. Calculations indicate that there was a very small amount of evaporation from the gasoline located in the sump that added to the vapor already present below the floating roof; however, this did not contribute significantly to the vapor concentration below the roof.

The addition of diesel to the tank would have displaced some of the gasoline vapor in the tank from below the floating roof to the space between the roofs, further enriching the flammable mixture above the floating roof.

ConocoPhillips Crude Oil Pipeline Operations

On the east side of the tank farm, a ConocoPhillips 12-inch-diameter crude oil pipeline was underground and aligned in a north-south direction. Near the east wall of the dike and between tanks 7 and 8, the overpressure protection piping for this pipeline was aboveground and inside the dike. The segment of this piping upstream of the rupture disk operated at the same pressure as the pipeline during normal operations. When the accident occurred, at 8:55 p.m. on April 7, the pipeline pressure at the pump discharge at Glenpool Terminal was about 1,348 psig. Between about 3:00 a.m. and 5:00 a.m. on April 8, the pressure was lowered to 550 psig. About an hour later, at 6:10 a.m., the heat from the fire weakened the flange assembly and isolation gasket, and the pipeline failed.

Operating Procedures

Explorer Procedures

Explorer's operating procedures and shipper information documents stated that deliveries from Explorer's pipeline system into tankage would be made at full line rate and that the tankage operator was responsible for eliminating conditions—such as filling new lines or filling tanks that have the floating roof on supporting legs after construction or repair—that may require a reduced flow rate.

Industry Recommended Tank Filling Rates

According to API RP 2003, for tanks that may contain a flammable mixture in the vapor space, such as can occur during switch loading, protective measures to control the electric charge in a storage tank include the following:

> Limit the fill line and discharge velocity of the incoming liquid stream to 1 meter/second (3 feet per second) until the fill pipe is submerged either two pipe diameters or 61 centimeters (2 feet), whichever is less. In the case of a floating roof (internal or open top) tank, observe the 1 meter/second (3 feet/second) velocity limitation until the roof becomes buoyant.

At the time of the explosion, the tee in the sump at the end of the fill pipe was submerged in the diesel by more than the recommended minimum depth, but the internal roof had not yet floated.

ConocoPhillips Tank Filling Rates

"Refined Product Tank Filling Rate Requirements" from the ConocoPhillips *Merged Terminal Operating and Procedures Guide* described the procedures and requirements for filling tanks. It addressed the prevention of static electricity charges between the refined product and the steel structure of the tank floor and appurtenances and concerns about the stability of floating roofs during tank filling.

For floating roof tanks, the ConocoPhillips guide defined an "empty tank" as any tank with the floating roof landed with vapor space between the roof and the surface of the product. The guide noted that, depending on the product, safety precautions may be applicable and environmental reporting requirements may exist.

The guide categorized refined products into three vapor-pressure groups (low-, intermediate-, and high-vapor-pressure) and referenced API RP 2003 as the source of this classification scheme. The guide provided examples of products in each group.

The guide stated that low-vapor-pressure products, such as diesel (No. 1 or No. 2), had the highest potential for static charge buildup. Also noted was that the introduction of low-sulfur forms of these products had caused greater concern because of the additional potential for ignition when static buildup occurs. The guide stated that delivery of low-vapor-pressure products into an empty tank should not exceed 3 feet per second until the surface of the liquid is above the fill nozzle by a distance of 2 feet or the equivalent of two pipe diameters, whichever is less. In the case of a tank with a floating roof, the 3-feet-per-second velocity limitation was to be observed until the roof became buoyant.[17] For intermediate-vapor-pressure products, it was noted that while there was some static electricity buildup in these products, reduced flow rates were not generally required unless the product was being handled in extreme temperature ranges. In this case, the intermediate-vapor-pressure products were to be handled like low-vapor-pressure products. For additional safety, the flow rate of intermediate-vapor-pressure products into empty tanks was to be limited to 3 feet per second whenever pipeline operating conditions permitted.

For high-vapor-pressure products, the ConocoPhillips procedures guide noted that while static buildup did occur in these products, the vapor space directly above the surface of the liquid was generally too rich with vapors to be ignited by static charges. For that reason, restricted flow rates were generally not required for these products. Gasoline was identified as a high-vapor-pressure product.

The guide also addressed the hazardous condition that may exist with a switch load when a low-vapor-pressure product, such as diesel, is pumped into a tank containing flammable vapors from a previous high- or intermediate-vapor-pressure product. When

---

[17] A 3-feet-per-second delivery velocity in the 30-inch fill line to tank 11 would have been equivalent to a flow rate of about 9,000 barrels per hour. The actual flow rate on April 7 was 27,492 barrels per hour (9.2-feet-per-second velocity in the fill line) at the beginning of the delivery. At this flow rate, the length of time it took to fill the sump with diesel was calculated to be less than 20 seconds. The flow rate at the end of the delivery was 20,409 barrels per hour (6.8-feet-per-second velocity in the fill line); the average delivery rate was 21,050 barrels per hour (7-feet-per-second velocity in the fill line).

high- or intermediate-vapor-pressure product is drained from a tank with a floating roof, air is pulled into the space below the roof, resulting in an air-gas vapor space. Once this condition exists, an explosion may occur if an ignition source, such as a buildup of static electricity, is present.

Postaccident Actions at ConocoPhillips Glenpool South Tank Farm

After the accident, tanks 7, 8, 9, and 12 were inspected, repaired as needed, and returned to service. Tanks 7, 8, and 12 were retrofitted by ConocoPhillips with two tees on the existing tee inside the sump with the intent of accommodating a higher flow rate from Explorer. Additionally, the splash plates over the sump openings were enlarged to cover the entire outline of the circular sumps. ConocoPhillips indicated that Tank 11 may be replaced depending on future operational requirements.

ConocoPhillips revised its operating procedures for the Glenpool South tank farm after the accident. The site-specific procedure, dated August 18, 2003, *Local Operating Procedures Guide for Glenpool South Pipeline and the Glenpool South Facility and Breakout Tankage*[18] *for ConocoPhillips,* states that when tanks are emptied and vacuumed to remove product from the bottom of the tank, the tank's roof will be refloated by pumping product from Glenpool Station before Explorer will deliver product into the tank and that Explorer will not deliver product into an empty tank (a tank where the roof is not floating). The procedure also identifies the static electricity hazard caused by movement of product in a pipe. To prevent a hazard, the velocity of product into any new tank, or the first filling of any tank that has been opened and gas-freed, must be maintained at or under 3 feet per second until the roof is floating. A table lists the allowable flow rates for a velocity in the fill pipe of 3 feet per second. A footnote to the table says that tank 12's two tees give "the delivery system sufficient design to accept [the] Explorer rate into the tank if the roof is not floating." The procedure does not identify switch loading or describe the hazards associated with switch loading.

In addition, ConocoPhillips prepared a procedure that requires tanks to be equipped with low level alarms and defines the minimum operating level for a tank. For tank 11, the minimum operating level would have been just above the level at which the roof legs touch the floor. The procedure identifies the conditions, such as taking a tank out of service for inspection or maintenance, for which the roof may be landed and instructs personnel that, for normal operations, operating a tank below the minimum operating level is not permitted.

---

[18] Federal regulations define a *breakout tank* as a tank used to relieve surges in a hazardous liquid pipeline system or to receive and store hazardous liquid transported by pipeline for reinjection and continued transportation by pipeline.

Federal Safety Regulations – Emergency Procedures

Federal regulations for hazardous liquid pipelines (49 *Code of Federal Regulations* (CFR) Part 195), which cover breakout tanks such as those at the Glenpool South tank farm, have requirements for emergency procedures, including emergency response planning and emergency response:

195.402 Procedural Manual for Operations, Maintenance, and Emergencies:

(a) General. Each operator shall prepare and follow for each pipeline system a manual of written procedures for conducting normal operations and maintenance activities and handling abnormal operations and emergencies. This manual shall be reviewed at intervals not exceeding 15 months, but at least once each calendar year, and appropriate changes made as necessary to insure that the manual is effective. This manual shall be prepared before initial operations of a pipeline commence, and appropriate parts shall be kept at locations where operations and maintenance activities are conducted. ...

(e) Emergencies. The manual required by paragraph (a) of this section must include procedures for the following to provide safety when an emergency condition occurs; ...(e)(2) prompt and effective response to a notice of each type of emergency, including fire or explosion occurring near or directly involving a pipeline facility, accidental release of a hazardous liquid ... from a pipeline facility, and operational failure ... and taking necessary action, such as emergency shutdown or pressure reduction, to minimize the volume of hazardous liquid ... that is released ... in event of a failure.

(e)(7) Notifying fire, police, and other appropriate public officials of hazardous liquid or carbon dioxide pipeline emergencies and coordinating with them preplanned and actual responses during an emergency, including additional precautions necessary for an emergency involving a pipeline transporting a highly volatile liquid.

Federal regulations for natural gas pipelines have similar requirements for emergency planning and response.

Industry Emergency Response Plan Guidance

For natural gas pipelines, the American National Standards Institute (ANSI) Gas Piping Technology Committee's Guide for Gas Transmission and Distribution Piping Systems[19] includes material intended to assist the user in complying with the Federal regulations. For emergency plans, it states:

---

[19] ANSI GPTC Z380.1, *Guide for Gas Transmission and Distribution Piping Systems,* Gas Piping Technology Committee. The Gas Piping Technology Committee is an independent consensus committee comprising representatives from the pipeline industry, including manufacturers, operators, and consultants, as well as from pipeline safety regulatory agencies.

Written procedures should state the purpose and objectives of the emergency plan and provide the basis for instructions to appropriate personnel. The objective of the plan should be to ensure that personnel who could be involved in an emergency are prepared to recognize and deal with the situation in an expeditious and safe manner. This may require that parts of the plan be developed and maintained in coordination with local emergency response personnel (e.g., police, fire, and other public officials) and with other entities in or near the pipeline rights-of-way (e.g., other utilities, highway authorities, and railroads) that may need to respond to a pipeline emergency.

For natural gas and hazardous liquid pipeline systems, the American Society of Mechanical Engineers (ASME) codes include requirements for emergency planning. However, the codes do not list electric utilities among the parties a pipeline operator should contact when planning its response to an emergency.

ConocoPhillips Emergency Procedures

The ConocoPhillips *Emergency Response Plan, Core Plan*, Volume 1, Section 5 ("Response Activities") and the *Oklahoma Emergency Response Plan*, "Response Zone Appendix (Glenpool Area)," specify actions to be taken in the event of an emergency. The plans are designed to ensure the safety of the public and company personnel when threatened by the release of hydrocarbons from a pipeline to the environment and to coordinate activities for prompt and safe repair of the pipeline.

The plan describes events that require immediate response, including receiving notices of an emergency, such as fire, explosion, or natural disaster involving pipeline facilities; release of hazardous liquids from a pipeline facility; or an operational malfunction causing a hazardous condition. For these situations, emergency shutdown procedures are specified: shut in the pipeline at the nearest block valves and notify the nearest pump station and/or the appropriate control center. The emergency procedures do not specifically include notifying nearby electric utilities, which in this case includes AEP.

Federal Safety Regulations – Ignition Protection

Title 49 CFR Part 195 prescribes safety standards and reporting requirements for pipeline facilities used in the transportation of hazardous liquids. These standards were amended on April 2, 1999 (Amendment 66). The amendment became effective on May 3, 1999, and incorporated by reference 13 consensus standards for aboveground steel storage tanks. One of the new requirements references API RP 2003 for the prevention of ignition from static electricity:

195.405(a)-- After October 2, 2000, protection provided against ignitions arising out of static electricity, lightning, and stray currents during operation and maintenance activities involving aboveground breakout tanks must be in accordance with API Recommended Practice 2003, unless the operator notes in the procedural manual (§195.402(c)) why compliance with all or certain provisions of API Recommended Practice 2003 is not necessary for the safety of a particular breakout tank.

Before this amendment, there were no specific regulatory requirements for aboveground tanks regarding protection against ignitions.

Tank Inspections

Office of Pipeline Safety

The Research and Special Programs Administration's Office of Pipeline Safety (OPS) provided inspection reports for the Glenpool South tank farm for the 5-year period before the accident. One inspection of tank 11 had been conducted in this period, on October 24, 2001, and was reported on a four-page form entitled *Breakout Tank Evaluation Form (Evaluation Report of Breakout Tank Facilities)*. The inspection of tank 11 was part of an overall inspection that evaluated five tanks at the Glenpool South tank farm and six tanks at Glenpool Terminal. For each tank, the first part of the evaluation form was completed; a single second part of the form was completed for the 11 tanks.

The first part of the evaluation form gathered factual information about the facility, such as tank size, specifications, and contents; cathodic protection data; availability of an Oil Pollution Act Response Plan; standards used for tank design, construction, and repairs; alarms; leak detection; dike description; firefighting equipment; signs; and security. The report included the following for tank 11: (1) there was an overfill alarm, (2) the tank bottom had no history of corrosion, (3) the tank bottom had cathodic protection, (4) the product stored was diesel, (5) the tank was constructed in accordance with API Standard 650 and inspected in accordance with API Standard 653, (6) there was an isolation valve on the tank inlet/outlet to isolate the tank from other facilities, and (7) no repairs, alterations, or reconstruction had taken place. It also noted that the capacity of the tank farm dike was 165,000 barrels, firefighting equipment was adequate, signs were adequate, and there was protection from vandalism and unauthorized entry. No noncompliances were noted.

The second part of the evaluation form listed the applicable regulatory requirements from 49 CFR Part 195 and had a space for the inspector to document his evaluation of each item as "S" (satisfactory), "U" (unsatisfactory), "N/A" (not applicable), and "N/C" (not checked). No noncompliances were noted. The inspector's documentation of his evaluation of ConocoPhillips' compliance with the requirements for prevention of static ignition (195.405(a)) was "N/A," indicating that the item was not inspected.

ConocoPhillips

In July 2000, tank 11 was externally inspected in accordance with API Standard 653 *(Tank Inspection, Repair, Alteration and Reconstruction)*. The inspection included an ultrasonic thickness survey, elevation survey, and visual inspection of the outside of the tank. Visible signs of rust and paint peeling in scattered areas around the entire tank were observed. The report recommended surface preparation, painting of these areas, and minor earthwork inside the dike to eliminate water accumulation. It also noted that the grounding system appeared to be in good condition. An internal inspection of tank 11 in accordance with API Standard 653 was scheduled for late 2003.

In API Standard 653, guidance for evaluation of a floating roof is given by referring the inspector to API Standard 650 *(Welded Steel Tanks for Oil Storage)* for external and/or internal floating roofs. In section H.4.1.6 ("Internal Floating Roofs"), this standard states:

> All conductive parts of the internal floating roof shall be electrically interconnected and bonded to the outer tank structure. This may be accomplished by electric bonding shunts in the seal area (a minimum of four, uniformly distributed) or flexible cables from the external tank roof to the internal floating roof (a minimum of two, uniformly distributed). The choice of bonding devices shall be specified by the purchaser, considering strength, corrosion resistance, joint reliability, flexibility and service life.

National Electrical Safety Code

The Institute of Electrical and Electronics Engineers, Inc., (IEEE) publishes the *National Electrical Safety Code*. The current edition is dated 2002. According to the IEEE, the code covers:

> basic provisions for safeguarding of persons from hazards arising from the installation, operation, or maintenance of (1) conductors and equipment in the electric supply stations, and (2) overhead and underground electric supply and communication lines. It also includes work rules for the construction, maintenance, and operation of electric supply and communication lines and equipment.

It is applicable to "the systems and equipment operated by utilities, or similar systems and equipment, of an industrial establishment or complex under the control of qualified persons." Specifically, the code covers utility facilities and functions up to the service point, which is the point of connection between the facilities of the serving utility and the premise wiring. The code does not include any guidelines or requirements for emergencies, such as emergency planning and response documents and training.

Analysis

No unusual or abnormal operating conditions were noted during the filling of tank 11 until the explosion occurred. A number of factors were found to have contributed to the explosion and fire and the impact of the fire on the community, and those factors are addressed in this analysis.

Exclusions

Various ignition sources were considered during the investigation. These included discharge of static electricity, lightning, electrical arcing, and human activity at the scene near tank 11 on the day of the accident. There was no known electrical weather activity on the night of the explosion. There was no evidence of electrical arcing in the junction box between tanks 11 and 12. The conduit from tank 11 to the box was filled with water, which would have prevented flammable vapors from being transmitted to the junction box and would have prevented a flame from being transmitted back to tank 11. In addition, no one was seen at or near the storage facility at the time of the explosion. Therefore, the Safety Board concludes that lightning, electrical arcing, and human activity near the tank did not cause or contribute to the accident.

Static Electricity and Prevention of Accidental Ignition at Storage Tanks

Investigators considered static electricity within tank 11 as a possible ignition source that led to the explosion. For static electricity to cause ignition, the following must be present: generation and accumulation of a static charge, a spark gap, and, in the spark gap, a flammable mixture and a static discharge of sufficient energy to cause ignition.

Static Charge Generation, Accumulation, and Dissipation

Static charge buildup in hydrocarbon liquids during transfer operations is a common occurrence. A static charge can be generated by the separation of liquid from a hose or nozzle, the movement of liquid in a pipe, or the mixing, pouring, agitating, misting, or splashing of liquid. The electric charge is carried with the flowing liquid into the downstream container or storage tank. The potential for and magnitude of the static charge increases with low-electrical-conductivity liquids, increased flow velocity, increased turbulence, the presence of water or other suspended particulates, turbulent contact of dissimilar fluids (such as water and a liquid hydrocarbon), and filtration. Static charges accumulate whenever the rate at which the charges are generated exceeds the rate at which the charges dissipate.

Materials with low electrical conductivity retain their electric charge longer than materials of higher conductivity. Explorer recovered a sample of the diesel that was transferred during the accident delivery. Laboratory analysis determined that the conductivity of the product was less than 1 pS/m. API RP 2003, *Protection Against Ignition Arising Out of Static, Lightning, and Stray Currents,* lists the range of conductivity for typical diesel as 0.5 to 50 pS/m and identifies any liquid with a conductivity of less than 50 pS/m as a static accumulator.

Explorer's operating agreement required customers to be able to receive product from Explorer's pipeline at full line rate. In the delivery piping system from Explorer's 28-inch pipeline to tank 11, Explorer operated a backpressure regulator to maintain a constant pressure at its custody transfer meter. Explorer and ConocoPhillips did not operate any equipment (except shutoff valves) at Glenpool to monitor or control the flow rate from Explorer.

As noted previously, API RP 2003 contains protective measures to control the generation of electric charge in a storage tank, including limiting the velocity of the liquid in the fill line and limiting the discharge velocity of the incoming liquid stream until the fill pipe inside the tank is covered to a specific depth. For tanks with an internal floating roof, it recommends that the velocity of liquid in the fill piping and the discharge velocity of the incoming liquid stream be limited until the internal floating roof has floated. During the initial stages of tank filling, more opportunity exists for the incoming stream to produce agitation or turbulence, hence the need to limit the incoming velocity. The velocity limitation for both measures is identified as 3 feet per second. At the time of the explosion, the tee in the sump at the end of the fill pipe was covered by more than the recommended minimum, but the internal roof had not yet floated.

The flow rate of diesel to tank 11 on April 7, 2003, initially ranged from a maximum of 27,492 barrels per hour to a minimum of 20,409 barrels per hour just before the explosion.[20] The Safety Board notes that for the entire 24-minute delivery the velocity of diesel in the tank 11 fill pipe was between 2.3 and 3 times the recommended maximum velocity of 3 feet per second. The tee at the end of the fill pipe in the sump reduced the effective discharge velocity of the incoming liquid streams to half that in the pipe; however, the tee did not change the upstream velocity in the fill piping. The Safety Board also notes that for the entire 24-minute delivery the velocity of diesel as it exited the tee was between 1.1 and 1.5 times the recommended maximum velocity of 3 feet per second. Although the tee decreased the exit velocity, it increased the turbulence as it redirected the incoming liquid by 90° inside the tee and then directed it against the sump walls in two places. A 6-foot by 12-foot rectangular splash plate centered on the sump covered the sump opening approximately 6 inches above the floor of the tank. Because the sump was 15 feet in diameter, this plate covered only about 40 percent of the sump and likely functioned to reduce, but not eliminate, splashing and misting of the diesel during the initial delivery.

---

[20] For liquid flow in the same size pipe, the flow velocity is proportional to the flow rate—if the flow rate is tripled, the flow velocity likewise increases by a factor of 3.

Thus, the Safety Board concludes that the high velocity of the diesel in the tank fill piping and the turbulence created in the sump area resulted in the generation of increased static charge and, combined with the very-low-electrical-conductivity (static accumulating) liquid, an elevated risk for a static discharge inside the tank.

Condition of Floating Roof Bonding System. The floating roof bonding system consisted of stainless steel wires whose ends were screwed to the top of the floating roof structure and attached to eyebolts on the underside of the fixed roof. Two of the four locations where the bond wires were connected to the floating roof were discovered in the wreckage. At these locations, the bond wires were intact and properly connected to the floating roof structure with screws.

Examination of the components in the Safety Board's Materials Laboratory showed that the coating on eyebolt No. 2 consisted of uniform layers of iron oxide typical of oxidation that occurs rapidly at elevated temperatures. Further, evidence of aluminum was found on the eyebolt threads, indicating that attached aluminum material, such as the grounding clip and aluminum nuts, had melted during the fire. The wire found at eyebolt No. 2 was looped around a steel bolt and embedded in solidified, melted aluminum. The wire at this location showed evidence of flattening, which was consistent with the wire having been connected to the aluminum grounding clip with a nut and bolt. Therefore, the available evidence indicates that the bonding wires were properly attached to the floating roof and the tank roof/shell. The Safety Board, therefore, concludes that the floating roof bonding system had most likely been installed as designed, and the available evidence was consistent with the components of the bonding system having been intact before the explosion.

Floating Roof Position and Spark Gap

When the draining of gasoline from tank 11 was completed at 5:33 p.m. on April 7, 2003, the floating roof landed and was supported by the legs. When the tank was filled with diesel at 8:35 p.m., the floating roof remained supported on the legs until the liquid level reached the pontoons underneath the roof deck. When the pontoons were submerged to approximately one-half of their diameter, the roof became buoyant. Because the floating roof was electrically bonded to the fixed roof and shell, once the diesel was in contact with the floating roof, the conditions necessary for a static discharge to occur between the diesel and the roof no longer existed.

Investigators determined the volume of diesel in the tank at the time of the explosion by using the volume that was metered by Explorer and adjusting for the volume delivered after the explosion, the volume that remained in the delivery piping, and the volume already in the sump. The volume in the tank at the time of the explosion was determined to be between 7,397 and 7,600 barrels. Based on the revised strapping table prepared by investigators, these volumes correspond to a height above the datum plate of about 3 feet 7 inches to 3 feet 9 inches.

Investigators determined that the surface of the charged diesel was within approximately 2 inches of the pontoons at the time of the explosion. This is the most likely time for a static discharge to occur. Hydrocarbon vapors such as those produced by gasoline require as little as 0.25 millijoules of energy for ignition. The energy in a static discharge can be much higher than this and yet not sufficient to leave a signature on the surface where the discharge occurred.

During the inspection of tank 12 at the Glenpool South tank farm, investigators noted that in one case, a drain tube extended slightly below the bottom of the pontoon. If this condition existed in the accident tank, the small-diameter drain tube could have increased the electric field strength when the statically charged diesel surface approached it. Depending on the magnitude of the static charge in the diesel, a static discharge could have occurred between the surface of the diesel and the drain tube, resulting in ignition of the flammable vapors.

Accident Switch Loading and Flammable Vapors

Operating records show that about 10:00 a.m. on April 4, as tank 11 was being drained, the level of gasoline in the tank dropped below that necessary to float the roof. When the draining operation ended, 4,994 barrels remained in the tank. The next day, April 5, between about 8:00 and 10:00 a.m., an additional 1,897 barrels of gasoline were added to the tank, but the total volume was still insufficient to float the roof. On April 6, about 3:00 a.m., a delivery of another 1,819 barrels of gasoline was begun that would bring the amount of gasoline in the tank to 8,710 barrels. During this delivery, at about 3:30 a.m., the gasoline in the tank reached a level sufficient to again float the roof. Thus, for more than 40 hours—from about 10:00 a.m. on April 4 until about 3:30 a.m. on April 6—gasoline vapor accumulated in the space between the surface of the gasoline and the floating roof. The gasoline introduced during the deliveries on April 5 and 6 displaced much of this vapor, which moved up through the two vents in the floating roof and, according to calculations, made the space between the fixed roof and the floating roof flammable. When the tank was subsequently drained dry, some of the vapor that had collected between the fixed roof and the floating roof was transferred back below the floating roof, resulting in a flammable environment below the floating roof as well.

The Safety Board concludes that the tank 11 operations from April 4 to 7, which included a partial draining that landed the floating roof and partial fillings before draining dry, allowed a large amount of gasoline vapor to be generated and distributed within the tank to create a flammable fuel-air mixture both above and below the floating roof.

The Safety Board, therefore, concludes that all the conditions necessary for fuel vapor ignition were present in the storage tank at the time of the accident, and the explosion most likely occurred when a static discharge ignited a flammable fuel-air mixture in the space between the surface of the diesel and the floating roof. The extensive damage to the tank is consistent with the flammable fuel-air mixture above the floating roof contributing to the force of the explosion.

ConocoPhillips' revised procedures do not address the effect of floating roof operations on both creation and prevention of a flammable atmosphere inside a tank. Because it is possible that a floating roof can be landed inadvertently, it is important to include procedures for eliminating or minimizing any flammable vapors that tank operations may have created. Therefore, the Safety Board believes that ConocoPhillips should revise its storage tank operating procedures to include instructions for minimizing the possibility of creating a flammable atmosphere and the occurrence of a static discharge inside a tank after a floating roof has been either intentionally or unintentionally landed, especially for tanks where switch loading is likely to occur. Because the height at which the legs are set and the height of product in a tank determine whether a roof is floating or landed, a pipeline operator's strapping table for a tank must be accurate to help operators determine the effect of tank operations on movement of the roof. Therefore, the Safety Board believes that the Research and Special Programs Administration should issue an advisory bulletin to liquid pipeline operators to validate the accuracy of their tank strapping tables.

No documentation was available for tank 11 regarding the design basis for the maximum flow rate into the tank, for sizing the piping connecting tank 11 to Explorer's facility, or for sizing the pipe discharge openings in the sump.

ConocoPhillips' current design procedures are based on API RP 2003. These procedures require that flow velocities be restricted in operating situations similar to those identified in API RP 2003. For flow velocity limitation in the case of a tank with a floating roof, the ConocoPhillips procedures stated that delivery of low-vapor-pressure products into an empty tank should not exceed 3 feet per second until the roof is buoyant. Discussions with ConocoPhillips personnel indicated that this statement of velocity limitation was applied to the velocity of the liquid as it exited the tee and not to the velocity of the liquid in the fill piping.

After the accident, ConocoPhillips retrofitted the fill piping in tanks 7, 8, and 12 so the fill piping system now terminates in two tees that result in four 30-inch-diameter openings inside the sump. This was done to accommodate higher flow rates from Explorer (up to Explorer's 28,200 barrels per hour ultimate capacity for diesel) and maintain a 3-feet-per-second maximum exit velocity from the tees. At 28,200 barrels per hour, the velocity in the 30-inch-diameter fill piping is 9.4 feet per second, and the exit velocity is 2.4 feet per second.

For tank 11 with a single tee, applying the velocity restriction only to the exit velocity from the tee allowed the velocity in the fill piping to exceed the API recommended maximum by a factor of 2. For the modifications to tanks 7, 8, and 12, the installation of two tees allows the velocity in the fill piping to exceed the API recommended maximum by a factor of 4. Increased flow velocity in the fill piping results in the generation of greater static charges, and when the product is a low-conductivity product (static accumulator), the excess static charge is transferred into the tank with the liquid. Addition of one or more tees at the end of the fill piping does not reduce the velocity of liquid in the fill piping.

The Safety Board concludes that ConocoPhillips operated in a manner that allowed tank 11 to be switch loaded at flow velocities significantly higher than those in both its own procedures and industry-recommended practices. The Safety Board believes that ConocoPhillips should evaluate its storage tank operating procedures and make the revisions necessary to ensure that product flow rates in both the tank fill line and the discharge nozzles are restricted to provide a level of protection against excess static electricity that is at least commensurate with industry standards.

Emergency Response

American Electric Power

The explosion occurred at about 8:55 p.m., and AEP was informed of the accident almost immediately. The transmission system operator knew that the AEP power lines were near the fire. An AEP representative visited the scene twice while the tank burned, and he inspected the power lines. But he did not notify the incident commander when he arrived on scene or inform him of his findings. About 5:52 a.m., one or more wires failed and fell onto the diked area, igniting another fire and causing the firefighting effort to be temporarily suspended.

An essential part of emergency response is the ability of the incident commander and his staff to be able to continually evaluate response options and determine the most appropriate actions. This requires that they have access to the most current information about not only the tank farm facilities and the products in the tank, but also of nearby facilities. The consideration is not only to minimize damage to these facilities, but also to prevent their involvement in the emergency, as such involvement may add unpredictability to the situation or cause the situation to escalate. Even though AEP knew almost immediately of the fire and the proximity of its power lines to it, the company responded only when asked. The fact that the AEP representative did not make contact with the incident commander limited the incident command's ability to keep AEP informed as the fire situation changed and limited AEP's knowledge of the situation. As a result, AEP's second response to the accident site was too late, and its overall response was ineffective. The Safety Board concludes that the AEP responder did not coordinate his actions with the incident command staff, and AEP did not take effective emergency action.

ConocoPhillips

On the east side of the tank farm, a ConocoPhillips 12-inch-diameter crude oil pipeline was underground. The overpressure protection piping for this pipeline was aboveground and inside the dike. When the accident occurred, the crude oil pipeline pressure at the pump discharge at Glenpool Terminal was about 1,348 psig. Between about 3:00 a.m. and 5:00 a.m. on April 8, the pressure was lowered to 550 psig. At 6:10 a.m., the heat from the fire weakened the flange assembly, and the pipeline failed. Crude oil sprayed out of the flange into the burning diesel and the nearby concrete fence and onto offsite property. By 6:17 a.m., ConocoPhillips had shut down the pipeline pump and closed the remotely operated valves in the pipeline.

As noted previously, Federal safety regulations require that a pipeline operator's emergency plan include procedures for

> prompt and effective response to a notice of each type of emergency, including fire or explosion occurring near or directly involving a pipeline facility, accidental release of a hazardous liquid ... from a pipeline facility, and operational failure ... and taking necessary action, such as emergency shutdown or pressure reduction, to minimize the volume of hazardous liquid ... that is released ... in event of a failure.

The ConocoPhillips emergency response plan stated that "shutting in the line at the nearest block valves" was to be initiated in response to these types of emergencies.

In this accident, ConocoPhillips did not shut down its nearby crude oil pipeline until after the segment of pressurized pipeline inside the dike had failed and leaked. Although the operating pressure was being reduced beginning 6 hours after the explosion, the magnitude of the tank 11 fire and the presence of the power lines and other ConocoPhillips tanks adjacent to the fire should have prompted the response specified in the ConocoPhillips emergency response plan. However, timely action by the ConocoPhillips controllers in Ponca City immediately after the pipeline failed minimized the release of oil into the fire.

Emergency Procedures

Because of the proximity of the AEP power lines and the Glenpool South tank farm, noted previously, it is obvious that damage, a failure, or an emergency at one facility had the potential to jeopardize the safety of the other. However, neither AEP personnel nor ConocoPhillips personnel had contacted one another to familiarize themselves with the affected facilities at the Glenpool South tank farm or to plan for a coordinated response to pipeline and electrical emergencies there.

At the Glenpool South tank farm, this recommendation for coordination with other entities would have applied to ConocoPhillips' coordination with AEP. After the tank exploded, ConocoPhillips initiated contact with AEP and requested that the electric lines be inspected. Although several AEP employees and the AEP transmission system operator were aware of the fire from television news reports, AEP did not respond to the emergency at the tank farm until specifically requested to do so by ConocoPhillips.

Had ConocoPhillips and AEP, as part of emergency planning, such as that described in the ANSI Guide for Gas Transmission and Distribution Piping Systems, previously met to discuss and plan emergency response activities for an electric line, tank, or pipeline emergency at the Glenpool South tank farm, it is likely that AEP's emergency response would have been more effective and that, considering the potential hazard to life and property, actions would have been taken to more thoroughly assess the threat to the electric lines and the consequences of their failure. The Safety Board concludes that because ConocoPhillips and AEP did not preplan their response to emergencies near the

Glenpool South tank farm, the emergency response was unsuccessful in managing the electrical hazard caused by the tank explosion and fire. The Safety Board believes that ConocoPhillips should revise its emergency response plan for the Glenpool South tank farm area and similar locations where ConocoPhillips facilities are near electric utilities to include preplanning with nearby electric facilities. The Safety Board believes that AEP should revise its emergency response plan to include areas, such as the ConocoPhillips Glenpool South tank farm, where pipeline transportation facilities are near AEP facilities, and include a requirement that the AEP emergency responders communicate and coordinate with the on-scene agency in charge.

As mentioned previously, Federal regulations for both hazardous liquid and gas pipelines require that pipeline operators have procedures for coordinating emergency response with fire, police, and other public officials. However, these regulations do not require pipeline operators to contact or coordinate with operators of other facilities, such as electric utilities, for emergency response. The Safety Board believes that the Research and Special Programs Administration should revise the emergency response planning requirements in the pipeline safety regulations to include coordination with electric and other utilities that may need to respond to a pipeline emergency.

ASME codes for gas and liquid pipeline systems include requirements for emergency planning, but they do not include electric utilities among the parties an operator should contact to preplan emergency responses. Therefore, the Safety Board believes that ASME should revise the emergency response planning requirements in its gas and hazardous liquid pipeline codes to include coordination with electric and other utilities that may need to respond to a pipeline emergency.

Regarding emergency planning guidelines for electric utilities, many States, including Oklahoma, have adopted the *National Electrical Safety Code* and require that operators of electric facilities within the scope of the code comply with its provisions. Other States have adopted all or part of the code or use its provisions as the basis for regulations. Nationally recognized codes are an important resource for facility operators. When written by Government and industry professionals with experience in emergency planning, implementation, and personnel training, a code can be a primary reference when an operator prepares a company-specific emergency plan. The *National Electrical Safety Code,* however, does not address emergency preparedness. Other industry codes applicable to major infrastructure include provisions for emergency planning and training (for example ASME B31.8, ASME B31.4, and NFPA 30).[21] The Safety Board concludes that comprehensive, practical industry guidance for the preparation of emergency plans would help operators of electric systems respond effectively to emergencies involving their utilities. The Safety Board, therefore, believes that the IEEE should revise the National Electrical Safety Code to establish requirements for operators to prepare and implement emergency response plans for electric facilities where an emergency may affect pipeline facilities or that may be affected by emergencies at pipeline facilities.

---

[21] ASME B31.8 (*Gas Transmission and Distribution Piping Systems*), ASME B31.4 (*Pipeline Transportation Systems for Liquid Hydrocarbons and Other Liquids*), and NFPA 30 (*Flammable and Combustible Liquids Code*).

Federal Oversight of Pipeline Operators

In the 5 years before the accident, the OPS conducted one inspection of the Conoco tank farms at Glenpool Terminal and the Glenpool South tank farm. This inspection occurred on October 24, 2001. Five tanks at the Glenpool South tank farm and six tanks at Glenpool Terminal were inspected, as evidenced by completion of a factual part of the inspection record form for each tank and one evaluation section of the inspection record form for all 11 tanks. Based on the Safety Board's review of other breakout tank inspection records, the OPS uses one set of the evaluation pages for multiple tanks in the same operating area of the same company.

One item included as a compliance requirement on the evaluation pages of the *Breakout Tank Evaluation Form* relates to this accident:

> 195.405(a) After October 2, 2000, protection provided against ignitions arising out of static electricity, lightning, and stray currents during operation and maintenance activities involving aboveground breakout tanks must be in accordance with API Recommended Practice 2003, unless the operator notes in the procedural manual (§195.402(c)) why compliance with all or certain provisions of API Recommended Practice 2003 is not necessary for the safety of a particular breakout tank.

The inspector's documentation of his evaluation of the ConocoPhillips breakout tanks for compliance with 49 CFR 195.405(a) was "N/A," which means that the tanks were not evaluated because the safety regulations were not applicable. Since these regulations became effective approximately 12 months before the inspection and the tanks at the Glenpool South tank farm were classified as "breakout tanks" subject to OPS jurisdiction, the determination that the regulations did not apply was obviously incorrect, and as a result, the October 24, 2001, safety evaluation of Conoco's tankage was incomplete.

Federal inspections of a pipeline operator should provide the operator with accurate feedback and the opportunity for immediate, constructive dialogue with the OPS. In addition, the OPS uses data obtained during field inspections to assess the effectiveness of its regulations and identify issues of operator noncompliance. In this case, since the inspector mistakenly determined that the regulatory requirements in the section of the *Breakout Tank Evaluation Form* related to prevention of ignition from static electricity were not applicable, the opportunity to review and evaluate Conoco's compliance with 49 CFR 195.405(a) for protections against ignition from static electricity was not taken, and there was no further review within the OPS.

Since 2002, the OPS has required that inspection reports be reviewed at the regional offices by a peer review team, a senior engineer, and/or the regional director. Before 2002, not all reports were reviewed. The purpose of the reviews is to ensure that each report has been completed properly, all required items have been addressed, and supporting evidence has been included. The reviews also allow the OPS to monitor the overall performance of the inspectors.

Conclusions

Findings

1. Lightning, electrical arcing, and human activity near the tank did not cause or contribute to the accident.

2. The floating roof bonding system had most likely been installed as designed, and the available evidence was consistent with the components of the bonding system having been intact before the explosion.

3. ConocoPhillips Company operated in a manner that allowed tank 11 to be switch loaded at flow velocities significantly higher than those in both its own procedures and industry-recommended practices.

4. The high velocity of the diesel in the tank fill piping and the turbulence created in the sump area resulted in the generation of increased static charge and, combined with the very low electrical conductivity (static accumulating) liquid, an elevated risk for a static discharge inside the tank.

5. Tank 11 operations from April 4 to 7, which included a partial draining that landed the floating roof and partial fillings before draining dry, allowed a large amount of gasoline vapor to be generated and distributed within the tank to create a flammable fuel-air mixture both above and below the floating roof.

6. All the conditions necessary for fuel vapor ignition were present in the storage tank at the time of the accident, and the explosion most likely occurred when a static discharge ignited a flammable fuel-air mixture in the space between the surface of the diesel and the floating roof. The extensive damage to the tank is consistent with the flammable fuel-air mixture above the floating roof contributing to the force of the explosion.

7. The American Electric Power responder did not coordinate his actions with the incident command staff, and American Electric Power did not take effective emergency action.

8. Because ConocoPhillips Company and American Electric Power did not preplan their response to emergencies near the Glenpool South tank farm, the emergency response was unsuccessful in managing the electrical hazard caused by the tank explosion and fire.

9. Comprehensive, practical industry guidance for the preparation of emergency plans would help operators of electric systems respond effectively to emergencies involving their utilities.

Probable Cause

The National Transportation Safety Board determines that the probable cause of the April 7, 2003, storage tank explosion and fire in Glenpool, Oklahoma, was ignition of a flammable fuel-air mixture within the tank by a static electricity discharge due to the improper manner in which ConocoPhillips Company conducted tank operations. Contributing to the extent of the property damage and the magnitude of the impact on the local community was the failure of American Electric Power employees to recognize the risk the tank fire posed to the nearby power lines and take effective emergency action.

Recommendations

As a result of its investigation of the April 7, 2003, explosion and fire in Glenpool, Oklahoma, the National Transportation Safety Board makes the following safety recommendations:

To the Research and Special Programs Administration:

Revise the emergency response planning requirements in the pipeline safety regulations to include coordination with electric and other utilities that may need to respond to a pipeline emergency. (P-04-07)

Issue an advisory bulletin to liquid pipeline operators to validate the accuracy of their tank strapping tables. (P-04-08)

To ConocoPhillips Company:

Revise your storage tank operating procedures to include instructions for minimizing the possibility of creating a flammable atmosphere and the occurrence of a static discharge inside a tank after a floating roof has been either intentionally or unintentionally landed, especially for tanks where switch loading is likely to occur. (P-04-09)

Evaluate your storage tank operating procedures and make the revisions necessary to ensure that product flow rates in both the tank fill line and the discharge nozzles are restricted to provide a level of protection against excess static electricity that is at least commensurate with industry standards. (P-04-10)

Revise your emergency response plan for the Glenpool South tank farm area and similar locations where ConocoPhillips Company facilities are near electric utilities to include preplanning with nearby electric facilities. (P-04-11)

To American Electric Power:

Revise your emergency response plan to include areas, such as the ConocoPhillips Company Glenpool South tank farm, where pipeline transportation facilities are near American Electric Power facilities, and include a requirement that the American Electric Power emergency responders communicate and coordinate with the on-scene agency in charge. (P-04-12)

To the Institute of Electrical and Electronics Engineers:

Revise the *National Electrical Safety Code* to establish requirements for operators to prepare and implement emergency response plans for electric facilities where an emergency may affect pipeline facilities or that may be affected by emergencies at pipeline facilities. (P-04-13)

To the American Society of Mechanical Engineers:

Revise the emergency response planning requirements in your gas and hazardous liquid pipeline codes to include coordination with electric and other utilities that may need to respond to a pipeline emergency. (P-04-14)

BY THE NATIONAL TRANSPORTATION SAFETY BOARD

ELLEN ENGLEMAN CONNERS
Chairman

CAROL J. CARMODY
Member

MARK V. ROSENKER
Vice Chairman

RICHARD F. HEALING
Member

DEBORAH A.P. HERSMAN
Member

Adopted: October 13, 2004

Appendix A

Investigation

The National Transportation Safety Board was notified on April 7, 2003, through the National Response Center, of a storage tank fire in Jenks, Oklahoma. The Safety Board dispatched an investigator from its Washington, D.C., headquarters. No Board Member accompanied the investigator. After the environmental cleanup around the tank was completed, additional investigators from Research and Engineering (Materials Laboratory and explosion/fire) and the pipeline group (SCADA) went to the site. No depositions or hearings were held in conjunction with the investigation. ConocoPhillips, Explorer Pipeline, the Research and Special Programs Administration's Office of Pipeline Safety, and the Glenpool, Oklahoma, Fire Department were parties to the investigation.

www.ingramcontent.com/pod-product-compliance
Lightning Source LLC
Chambersburg PA
CBHW080918290526
45795CB00007BA/2560